Light Bulbs Exploding

"Practical! *Light Bulbs Exploding* provides a clear, concise, and easy-to-follow and understandable approach to the who, what, when, why, how, and benefits of using modified inductive Bible studies. The book explains how this approach can be transformative in people's lives as they interact with God's Word, the Holy Spirit, others, and prayer. It also includes two suggested outlines for Bible studies using the books of 1 John and Malachi."

—MARK LOWREY
Founder, Reformed University Fellowship (RUF)

"As one of the University of Florida students who was in the first inductive Bible study that Rod taught there almost forty years ago, I profited immensely from being under his knowledge and teaching. I realize as I am reading this book that my own personal Bible study, as well as the methods and ideas that I use when I lead Bible-study groups, stem largely from the teaching and methods I learned way back then as a new believer and student of the Word! I highly endorse this book for those who want to study the Bible and lead others into understanding its truths."

—WENDY HOWELL THOMAS
Reformed University Fellowship (RUF) Participant

"I have known Rod for over forty-five years . . . fifty-five counting little league baseball. Working together as RUF campus ministers, it was our firm conviction that small-group Bible studies were/are the lifeblood of a campus ministry. We have since discovered the same is true of the local church. I wish I had this book in hand years ago. Rod helps the reader to understand both the importance of modified inductive Bible study and the tools needed to be an effective Bible-study leader. *Light Bulbs Exploding* needs to be in the hands of every pastor and church leader wanting their people to experience the Bible coming alive in a small-group context."

—HAL FARNSWORTH
Founder of RUF at Vanderbilt University

"The practical benefit of this work is in the application of the principles to the books of 1 John and Malachi. The principles and structure of the modified inductive method of Bible study are clearly demonstrated with a model that can be followed."

—**RICHARD P. BELCHER JR.**
Reformed Theological Seminary

Light Bulbs Exploding

Illuminating Small Group Bible Study

Rod Culbertson

WIPF & STOCK · Eugene, Oregon

LIGHT BULBS EXPLODING
Illuminating Small Group Bible Study

Copyright © 2021 Rod Culbertson. All rights reserved. Except for brief quotations in critical publications or reviews, no part of this book may be reproduced in any manner without prior written permission from the publisher. Write: Permissions, Wipf and Stock Publishers, 199 W. 8th Ave., Suite 3, Eugene, OR 97401.

Wipf & Stock
An Imprint of Wipf and Stock Publishers
199 W. 8th Ave., Suite 3
Eugene, OR 97401

www.wipfandstock.com

PAPERBACK ISBN: 978-1-6667-0871-4
HARDCOVER ISBN: 978-1-6667-0872-1
EBOOK ISBN: 978-1-6667-0873-8

10/25/21

Unless otherwise indicated, Scripture quotations are from the Holy Bible, English Standard Version (ESV), copyright © 2001 by Crossway, a publishing ministry of Good News Publishers. Used by permission. All rights reserved.

Scripture quotations from the (NASB®) New American Standard Bible,® copyright © 1960, 1971, 1977, 1995, 2020 by the Lockman Foundation (www.lockman.org), are used by permission. All rights reserved.

Dedication

WITH GREAT GRATITUDE FOR his godliness, humility, giftedness as a teacher of the things of God, and kindness extended to me when I was a fledgling seminary student at Columbia International University (Columbia Graduate School of Bible and Missions in that day), I wish to dedicate this book to the late Dr. William Larkin, New Testament scholar, author, and friend, who not only served CIU well for years but served me personally, along with hundreds of other CIU students and Bible students around the world. He listened to me express my struggles during that challenging first year of seminary in the fall of 1977, and he taught me to love Greek, to understand its usefulness, and to utilize it in my ministry. He exposed me to everything contained in the New Testament, except for the Gospels, and I well remember the diligence required to master the material he covered in his courses. A quiet man who maintained an even disposition, Dr. Larkin was not a man lacking in conviction. He had a strength of character that enabled him to teach with firmness, and yet he reflected the warmth and diplomacy of the evangelical pluralism that distinguishes CIU as an institution. While I was a student, he helped me navigate the world of Presbyterianism and even took me to a presbytery meeting. He once drove two hundred miles round trip one Sunday to hear me preach my third sermon ever—just because he was interested in me. Dr. Larkin was loyal to me after I graduated from CIU (MDiv) and moved on to learn the ropes of real ministry with Reformed University Fellowship (RUF) at the University of Florida. We corresponded over the years, and staying in touch led to a constant, though intermittent, friendship that grew through time. Eventually, after I joined Reformed Theological Seminary in Charlotte, I was permitted to call him Bill, which confirmed a friendship that would last a lifetime. Sadly, he declined quickly in his late sixties and my mentor was gone—too early for me. Nevertheless, the great gift he gave me—beyond seeing his love for Christ, his family, and his school—was the pleasure and joy of hermeneutics, better known as the science of biblical interpretation. I fell in love with Greek exegesis, diagramming sentences, sermon preparation, and teaching the text. The art of properly handling the word of God using the original Greek text was essential to the decades of expository preaching and teaching that has characterized my ministry. This book, *Light Bulbs Exploding*, is certainly a small piece of fruit that was harvested from the fertile tree of Bill Larkin's classroom instruction. I hope that this work will be both engaging and beneficial to others as they disciple believers in exploring the word of God through both inquiry and the detailed excavation of truth. May the Lord use it to grow his kingdom by his Holy Spirit's power. Bill Larkin would like that!

Contents

Illustrations | ix

Acknowledgments | xi

Introduction | xiii

1. The Modified Inductive Bible Study Method | 1
   Expanded Explanation

2. Lesson Planning: The Art of Asking Questions | 9
   Questioning the Text: Modified Inductive Bible Study

Appendix One: Disciple Investing through Modified Inductive Bible Study (MIBS) | 31
   Working through the Book of First John

Appendix Two: Disciple Investing through Modified Inductive Bible Study | 116
   Working through the Book of Malachi

Bibliography | 165

Illustrations

Figure 1: Subject/Learner/Teacher Paradigm | 13

Figure 2: Bloom's Taxonomy | 20

Figure 3: From Mystery to the Light of Christ (1 John 2:9) | 54

Figure 4: Overcoming Faith (1 John 5:4) | 103

Acknowledgments

WITH MUCH GRATITUDE, I want to thank my hardworking and enthusiastic RTS teaching assistant, Katie Larson, for her faithful efforts in proofing and editing the text, as well as organizing all of the necessary requirements to make publishing this book possible. I certainly could not have accomplished this work without her. I also want to thank Mr. Chris Chaney, who read through the book and gave me some positive feedback from a layperson's standpoint. I must also thank my beloved wife, Cathy, who allowed me to hide out in the mountains alone while I perfected the finished product. She supports me in every way possible. And finally, I thank the Lord Jesus Christ, who called this sinner to follow him and who has faithfully led the way as I heeded his call almost fifty years ago. To God be the glory.

Introduction

How Dr. Robert Traina Changed My Life and Ministry

Serendipitous Discovery

Many years ago, as I was in the final semester of my seminary career, I came across a book that I discovered on sale in the campus bookstore. I believe it was an unused new book in the used book section of the store. The title of the book was *Methodological Bible Study,* and the author was a seminary professor by the name of Dr. Robert Traina. Dr. Traina (1921–2010) was professor emeritus of biblical studies and, for nearly ten years, had been dean of the seminary and vice president for academic administration at Asbury Theological Seminary in Wilmore, Kentucky.

Asbury has historically been known as a Bible- and Christ-honoring school in the Wesleyan tradition. Now, I would readily admit that this book isn't for everyone. However, when I first read it in seminary, I found it quite engaging. It is primarily a book on hermeneutics or the topic of biblical interpretation. The book assists the reader in learning how to approach the Bible without presuppositions. In other words, Dr. Traina trains a student of the Bible to look at God's word afresh, as if for the first time ever. I personally give a five-star rating to the book, because it set the foundation for both my college ministry and my study of the Bible throughout the rest of my life. I am not exaggerating its influence, especially in my own ministry. *Methodological Bible Study* honed my skills of personal Bible study and helped me to develop materials for small group Bible study leadership. I believe that the serious Bible student will love this book, especially one who is interested in the science of interpreting the Bible. Of course, I am biased.

Introduction

Nevertheless, the lessons I learned from Dr. Traina's *Methodological Bible Study* became very relevant when I entered full-time ministry, particularly as I served in my first few years as a campus minister for Reformed University Fellowship (RUF) at the University of Florida. Some biographical explanation might be appropriate at this juncture. My wife, Cathy, and I moved from Columbia, South Carolina, to Gainesville, Florida, in July 1980. It was in Gainesville that I had to take the theory of seminary and apply it to practice. And as they say, "They didn't teach me *that* in seminary!" Small group Bible study leadership was not a part of my seminary training. Of course, seminary can't cover everything a minister needs to know. Professional ministry education is clearly only one facet of the disciple investing process. I certainly have a high view of seminary training, especially when it is based on a Christ-centered, Bible-centered, and Bible-believing curriculum. Seminary invests in the student, and the student invests in others as a result of the benefits of seminary. Hopefully, everyone involved in the process loves the Lord and is following Jesus as a disciple. Nevertheless, seminary does not fully prepare its graduates for the task of doing campus ministry, and I truly was confronted with that reality as a first-year campus minister.

Ironically, on that winter day in my seminary bookstore, early in 1980, *Methodological Bible Study* was just a book I picked up on a whim. It was not an assigned text or necessary reading for any of my courses. Call me crazy, but facing a full load of courses, including Hebrew, all of the course requirements (papers and exams), and an internship in a local church, while also being a newlywed of six months, I read Traina in my free time—sort of like a seminary hobby or outlet. Yes, some would say I was a bit imbalanced and over the top in my seminary world, and that was probably true. Nevertheless, looking back, I wonder, "How could it be possible that I might earn a master of divinity degree in a program that didn't include Traina as a required textbook? How could I survive ministry without this life-changing book?" Possibly I might have picked up more basic hermeneutical training somewhere else along the line, but Traina was a ministry-transforming volume for me. At least, I soon discovered that it could and would be.

Introduction

Failure Leads to Discovery

After graduating from seminary in June 1980, I would soon start my ministry with University of Florida (UF) students. However, honestly assessing the situation, I really didn't know what I was doing during the first year of my labors at UF. Previously, I had been the recipient of multiple avenues and sources of disciple investing prior to coming to faith in Christ. And after I became a Christian, many people invested in my walk with the Lord, including two or three campus ministries. As far as trying to reach UF students, I attempted some Campus Crusade (Cru)-based ministry and some Navigator-type ministry, with a little InterVarsity Christian Fellowship methodology thrown in. I engaged in these collaborated efforts undergirded by a theological foundation based on Reformed theology and an emphasis on the local church. Without going into details, my first year of ministry after stepping right off the seminary campus was a disaster. The only positive accomplishments were that I was still happily married (mostly) and the Lord raised the necessary funds for our ministry (that was huge and memorable!). The students with whom I worked led two small groups, but I did not have even one to lead myself. My large group meeting developed into a small group meeting. I did plan a number of one-to-one appointments, meeting with older students, newer students, non-Christian students, and many cold contacts in order to try to build up the group. I also made a lot of church and Christian school contacts. Finally, however, at the end of my first year on campus, I had what appeared to be a breakthrough in this difficult first year of ministry.

A somewhat fundamentalist Christian high school in Pensacola, Florida, responded to one of my requests asking for any student contacts they may know of who were attending UF. It appeared that I hit the mother lode with this response. The school sent me the names of three freshmen students who, to the school's knowledge, had not found a church in Gainesville or any type of campus ministry at UF. They all lived in the same dorm; two of them were roommates. Plus, they were all professing Christians (of course, that often doesn't mean much, even in fundamentalist circles), so surely they would want solid Christian fellowship. When one of their mothers heard about my interest, she actually called me to tell me how grateful she was that I was interested in these boys! Out of the blue, in the middle of the spring, just before the last quarter of the year (UF was not on the semester system yet), I contacted these three young men. Amazingly, they not only met with me (which often didn't happen), but were actually willing to attend a small group Bible study that I was going to begin. On top of that, they allowed me to hold it in their own dorm room. I even found and invited a couple of other new, freshmen contacts to attend. I was truly excited about the possibilities.

But the question in my mind remained: What will I do with them? What will we study? What materials will we use? Unbelievably, looking back, I fell into default mode. Taking the easiest route and probably one of the worst routes possible for guys raised in a fundamentalist Christian school environment much of their lives, I turned to a very basic fill-in-the-blank booklet developed by the Navigator ministry. The *Design for Discipleship* series was very familiar to me since I had seen it in my own college freshman experience. The *Design for Discipleship* series, though useful and helpful, requires preparation by the student (certainly not a bad idea but mostly good in theory only, I discovered). It studies topics in an organized fashion, primarily looking at various passages of Scripture out of context, all the while teaching the learner the basics of the Christian life—and of course using a simple fill-in-the-blank method. I knew that God had used the series in my own life and recognize that he has used it in the lives of many others (and will continue to use it). However, using this method while holding a weekly Bible study with these five young freshmen UF students became like a visit to the dentist—painful for all participants and observers alike! They tended not to prepare, felt guilty for not preparing, met with me in true legalistic and perfunctory fashion, said and discussed hardly anything, displayed little enthusiasm, listened to me talk, endured our meetings, and overall appeared regularly bored. (After all, it was springtime in the afternoon in Florida—what would *you* rather be doing?) The happiest I ever saw them was when the semester and the school year ended and the small group study was finally over. Needless to say—and sad to say—when they returned to UF in the fall, they didn't come running to me for more "dynamic, life-changing" small group Bible study meetings. As a matter of fact, I don't think that I saw or heard from any of them ever again!

Help!

In the meantime, through a handful of referrals, I had connected with Reverend Mr. Mark Lowrey, the coordinator and founder of Reformed University Ministries (RUM, now more commonly known as RUF) who resided in the state of Mississippi. He became a very helpful distant advisor.

Introduction

And because I could not attend the upcoming RUF summer staff training held in Jackson, Mississippi due to the impending birth of our first child, Reverend Lowrey (I'll call him Mark) came to visit me in Gainesville. He gave me one week of condensed staff training in a period of forty-eight hours of non-stop talking (with the exception of sleep), with Cathy and I *mostly* listening! It was so very enlightening and helpful. And as we talked about my numerous failures during the first year of ministry, he frequently spoke about the importance of having a philosophy of ministry, how that philosophy applies to the college campus, and how RUF uses small group Bible studies as a part of its philosophy of ministry. He said, "What we like to do is to get the students to open the Bible and read it—some for the first time ever—and then study it for what it says. We just pick a short book of the Bible and study it verse by verse in a modified inductive study method." What a revelation this statement seemed to me! And although I had the hermeneutical (interpretative) skills to study the Bible in this manner, I had never been through anything comparable in any previous ministry or church experience. Thankfully, I had been trained in the skill and art of expository preaching, so I had that basic commitment in my ministry arsenal. However, as Mark described this method of Bible study, the first thing that came to my mind was the book that I had scoured and devoured a little over one year earlier: "Traina!" "I can take the principles set forth in Traina," I thought, "and walk through a book of the Bible with my students" (assuming, of course, I had any students; as I said, it was a rough first year).

God Was at Work!

The next few months were an adventure. Without going into details, the Lord started sending us incoming freshmen, some with incredible stories and some through unique circumstances. Their stories were answers to a lot of people's prayers. By the fall, I had found (or been given) ten new committed freshmen students in addition to the twenty or so returning upperclassmen and graduate students with whom we were working. I knew that the future of the ministry would be derived from investing (what I call disciple investing) in the lives of these freshmen students. We did not have a large group meeting (I had abandoned it after its demise in the spring of the first year) so I simply told these students that I was going to begin a freshman small group Bible study. One of the students opened up her dorm room and, sitting on two beds, two dorm room chairs, and the floor, we had eight to ten students meeting together on a weekly basis. This group of eager students was a thrilling experience for me, especially after all my first-year failures. I was exuberant, and the best was yet to come.

First John

Let me give a little background on the book that I chose to study with these freshmen students. During my last year of college, I had decided to try to do some extensive Scripture memory work. Someone had told me that the book of 1 John was a simply written book and would therefore be an easy book to try to memorize. I don't know if it was any easier to memorize than any other book, but I spent the summer before my last semester of college (I went one extra fall semester due to changing majors during my sophomore year at the University of South Carolina) working on memorizing the book of 1 John. Each weekend, I set aside a couple of hours on Saturday to memorize the book. It was arduous work, and my mother would take the time to help me review everything I had memorized.[1] Essentially, as I memorized the book of 1 John, I fell in love with it. I continued to study it on my own prior to seminary, eventually making an outline chart for the contents and flow of the book just for fun. (I don't have it memorized anymore—I couldn't keep up with the weekly reviews—but I am still very familiar with its contents). So, when I was able to pull these freshmen UF students together for a small group Bible study, I had fallen in love with the book so much that 1 John was my obvious book of choice to use with them.

Therefore, that second fall semester of my early tenure at UF, I focused on studying the book of 1 John and turning my study into a modified inductive small group Bible study designed for college-age students. Without explaining the many principles included in methodological Bible study (some of that is below), I would simply say that what Dr. Traina taught me was to come to the text as if you had never read it before. Then, to observe the words, sentences, phrases, and context of the passage. One must learn the background of the book and ask the natural questions that any person who had never seen the passage would ask. My plan was to divide the book of 1 John into fourteen teaching sections for a college semester (UF was now thankfully on the semester system—a schedule that was much more

---

1. Somewhat like the classic video of Andy Griffith helping Deputy Barney Fife recite the preamble to the United States Constitution. If you need a visual of what I am talking about, see the video on YouTube.

conducive to campus ministry), prepare the questions each week (questions based solely on the text), and then guide the students as we walked through the book. Now, I must say that the Holy Spirit was obviously working among these students as well as through this small group format. I think the method of study was, without question, far more effective than what I had attempted just a few months prior during the spring quarter with five reluctant freshmen male participants. I also think that prayer was an underlying reason for any of the effectiveness that arose. Nevertheless, the interaction of student with text and student with student was a powerful dynamic. God had brought and prepared these students for this time and place. They wanted to grow in Christ, grow together, and truly understand the Bible and its implications for their lives.

Added Dynamic

I discovered that the dynamic of the modified inductive Bible study method is the key to the personal, intellectual, and spiritual growth that this approach to the Scriptures brings to its participants. The interaction provided by the means of fostering an atmosphere of discussion is irreplaceable. This method should not fall prey to the common accusation that is so often leveled at small group Bible study discussions, i.e., "Small group Bible study discussions are the pooling of ignorance!" Personal opinion and personal expression do matter, hence the dynamic. However, the conscientious modified inductive Bible study group has at hand a competent, trained, and knowledgeable leader who is capable of making certain that the focus of the discussion is on the passage to be considered. This leader has done the homework, studied and knows the passage well, and has developed questions that are drawn from the verses, as well as the material of the passage. If necessary, this individual could teach the material didactically (lecture-style). But the point is that neither the teacher nor the students predominate the passage. Rather, the passage is the subject at hand, and the method involves analysis by learners who have an expert (the teacher) in their midst. Yes, the teacher guides the discussion, restrains the rabbit trail distractions, and maintains the focus of the study, all the while making every effort to allow the students to grapple with the Scripture text.

If you are interested in pursuing the use of the modified inductive Bible study method and learning more about the science of this approach to disciple investing, please take note of the next section of this work. The

INTRODUCTION

following material includes some of the helpful highlights gleaned from Dr. Traina's book *Methodological Bible Study* and some additional suggestions beyond Dr. Traina's text. And the appendices include two different examples, one from the Old Testament (Malachi) and one from the New Testament (1 John), of the questioning approach that walks through an entire short book of the Bible in an inductive manner.

1

The Modified Inductive Bible Study Method

Expanded Explanation

Some Basic Hermeneutical Considerations

BEFORE I EXPLAIN THE science and the art of the modified inductive Bible study method, I would like to provide some of the basic interpretational principles that I derived from Dr. Traina.[1] I have listed these principles in bare skeletal form, but there should be enough information to assist the reader in gaining the general idea of focus and purpose.

Basic Interpretation Principles

Here are some basic hermeneutical considerations that one must give to the selected text, passage, paragraph, or book of the Bible:

1. Look at the authorship, background of the book, purpose, and the situation (or problem) that the book is addressing. "The task of re-creating the minds and purposes of authors who wrote hundreds of

---

1. Traina, *Methodological Bible Study*.

years ago is a very complex one, and at times one cannot be sure that one has succeeded."[2]

Example

In the letter of 1 John, the apostle John is writing to a broad audience (considered to be a general audience of early church believers) and is helping them to deal with heresies of either pre-gnostic or gnostic origins. The student of the text needs to consider the impact that those heresies might have upon the original audience.

The two primary heresies of first-century gnosticism were:

1. Cerinthianism: This heresy emphasized pleasure and licentiousness (freedom of the flesh); it demonstrated a libertine spirit—the flesh is evil, but it doesn't matter what the flesh does as long as the spirit is right. Cerinthianism denied that God, being a pure spirit, would unite himself to a human, physical body. Therefore, Christ was not both God and man.

2. Docetism: God can't be known; Christ didn't really live in his body; it just seemed that way. God can't die (his spirit came upon Jesus at his baptism and departed prior to his death on the cross).

How do these heresies bear upon the purpose of John's letter? Notice 1 John 1:1–3 and the emphasis on an actual experience with the real, human Jesus.

2. Read the text as if you have never read it before. "When reading the Scriptures, one ought to put nothing into them, but rather draw everything from them and suffer nothing to remain hidden which is really in them."[3]

Example

Think about reading any of the four Gospel narratives as if you have never even heard the name of Jesus before. Imagine that you had grown up on a secluded island and an airplane flew over and dropped

---

2. Traina, *Methodological Bible Study*, 54–55.
3. Traina, *Methodological Bible Study*, 11.

down a Gospel account in your own language. You've never seen it before. Think of the first-century readers of and/or listeners to the stories of Jesus for the first time ever. What would they think or conclude? These are unbelievable stories written as truths to be believed!

3. Look for relationships.

   A. "Examine all connections closely, but especially conjunctions, prepositional phrases, and subordinate clauses."[4]

   B. Look for relationships: micro to macro.

      1. Words
      2. Phrases
      3. Clauses
      4. Sentences
      5. Paragraphs
      6. Segments
      7. Subsections
      8. Sections
      9. Divisions
      10. Books
      11. The entire Bible (historical redemptive considerations and biblical theology)[5]

Examples

What is the significance of the word *but* in Eph 2:4?

What is the word *therefore* there for in Rom 8:1?

How does a particular book of the Old Testament testify of (or tell us about) Christ?

How does a particular book of the New Testament testify of Christ?

---

4. Traina, *Methodological Bible Study*, 63.
5. Traina, *Methodological Bible Study*, 36–37.

4. Ask yourself these questions:

    A. What is here?
    B. Why is it here?
    C. Why is it where it is?
    D. What difference would it make if it were omitted?
    E. What difference would it make if it were elsewhere?[6]

Examples

Why do we need the book of 1 Thessalonians?

What doctrines or truths of the Christian faith might be missing if we did not have the book of 1 Thessalonians?

Note to Leader

These are some challenging questions for the modified Bible study leader. He or she will have to do some extra study in order to know the answers.

5. Observation of atmosphere.

    Definition: "The underlying tone or spirit of a passage, which though intangible is nevertheless real."[7]

    Notice moods that characterize a passage, for example, despair, thanksgiving, awe, urgency, joy, humility, or tenderness. It is my opinion that moods and emotional tone are very helpful categories by which to elicit a response from the student. Get the reader to discern the emotional state or influence of the writer and/or hearers of the story or content.

---

6. Traina, *Methodological Bible Study*, 66.
7. Traina, *Methodological Bible Study*, 71.

The Modified Inductive Bible Study Method

Example

The apostle Paul becomes very personal in his second letter to the church at Corinth, due to the necessity of defending his apostleship against attackers who are undermining his authority among the believers at Corinth. Take note of his passion and emotion as it is displayed throughout the epistle.

Example

Note the crescendo of emotion at the end of Rom 8 as Paul contemplates the wonder of God's great love and also at the end of Rom 11 as he contemplates the wonderful plan of God for both the Gentiles and Israel.

6. Use of the imagination. "The imagination may supply the magic carpet which transports us to biblical times and enables us to think and live and feel with the writers and characters of Scripture."[8]

   Example

   It is rather easy to imagine the scene in which Peter heals the lame man in Acts 3: "And leaping up, he stood and began to walk, and entered the temple with them, walking and leaping and praising God." But also think of what it must have been like to be the paralyzed man who was lowered through the roof of a house in the midst of a crowd of people. How do you think the man looked? How about the onlookers in the crowd? They were indeed "all amazed and glorified God, saying, 'We never saw anything like this!'" How about the scribes who were cynical about Jesus's power to forgive? And what about the homeowner who had his roof violated? What did this scene look like?

7. Interpretive questions

   A. Term-al (the use of terms) questions: Note the use and significance of the terminology that the author uses to make the point.

---

8. Traina, *Methodological Bible Study*, 94.

Example

"What is meant by the term 'glorify' in the context of John 17?"

"What is involved in Jesus being glorified?"[9]

B. Structural questions: Note structural relations of contrast and comparison.

NOTE TO LEADER

I think this observation is one of the most helpful in assisting the learner to think through the author's intent.

Example

What is meant by contrasting God's ways and thoughts to man's ways and thoughts (Isa 55:8–9)? How are they different?

C. Form-al (the use of literary form) questions: Why is this literary form used in general, and why in this particular instance? Literary form would include the following possibilities: history/epic, narrative (story—gospel/literal/symbolic), law (ethical instruction), wisdom literature, poetry, psalm, prophecy, epistle (letter), apocalyptic (prophetic revelation), biography, discourse (speech/sermon/prayer), parable/allegory, drama.

Example

Does the literature (storytelling form) of Genesis appear to be mythological, symbolical, poetical, or historical and literal in nature? How would the original audience (Israel preparing to enter the promised land) understand the story? How do Jesus and Paul handle the narratives when they cite the respective passages from Gen 1–11 specifically?

---

9. Traina, *Methodological Bible Study*, 99.

D. Atmospheric question: tone and mood. What is the author's state or frame of mind? What has triggered or precipitated this mood?

   Example

   Notice Paul's incredulity and exclamations in the book of Galatians, as he expresses astonishment at the wavering faith of these beloved believers (Gal 1:6; 2:17; 3:1; 4:19–20; 5:12; 6:11–17). What emotions do you see in these passages? Why is his tone so emotional in his communication to the Galatians? What points is he trying to make?

8. Application

   A. Personal (self) application and application to others
   B. Application to present spiritual, social, economic, and political realities
   C. Application to present local, national, and universal situations
   D. Application to believers and non-believers
   E. Application to ethics, theology, Christian practice, and sanctification[10]

   Examples

   How do the Beatitudes of Matt 5:1–10 impact my personal life?

   Which of the Beatitudes impacts me the most personally? Why?

   Which of the Beatitudes would likely change the culture in our church? Why?

   Which of the Beatitudes is most needed in our nation's culture? Why?

   If you could promote just one of the Beatitudes through worldwide satellite or other media, in order to impact every person and nation in the world, which one would you choose? Why?

   Choose one ethical issue that believers face and explain how any one beatitude might impact them.

---

10. Traina, *Methodological Bible Study*, 216.

Significance

Although all of the information mentioned above may appear overwhelming, once the Bible study leader walks or works through the selected passage with these thoughts in mind, the questions will become more relevant and vital. And, of course, the leader does not have to ask every question of the specific text; but the more the leader studies, the more the text will come to life. And that life will be communicated to the group as they participate in the modified inductive Bible study process. Hopefully the examples provided in this section will give the reader/leader an idea of how to analyze a given Scripture passage from the various perspectives addressed above.

2

Lesson Planning: The Art of Asking Questions

Questioning the Text: Modified Inductive Bible Study

Deduction versus Induction

As we consider the method of modified inductive Bible study, a few words of explanation are necessary. First, let me provide a brief definition of deductive and inductive reasoning.

Deductive Reasoning

Simply stated, *deduction* or *deductive reasoning* begins with a statement or a point of argument and then provides further statements in order to validate or prove the original premise. A sermon or speech would normally follow a deductive approach. The individual presenting the argument is constructing or building the argument logically.

Here is an example of deductive reasoning:

Statement: Jesus is the Son of God.

Fourfold proof/logic that Jesus is the Son of God (more could be provided):

1. Jesus's miracles over every domain of human life prove that he is the Son of God.
2. Jesus forgives sin, and only God can forgive sin.
3. Jesus's seven "I am" statements in the gospel of John are based on Yahweh's name, "I am," found in Exod 3:14, implying that Jesus, too, is the great "I am."
4. Jesus claims, "I and the Father are one."

Essentially, the arguer has made a forceful declaration or statement of fact and then built a case, through the statement of (hopefully) convincing proofs to validate the original declaration or premise.

Inductive Reasoning

On the other hand, *inductive reasoning* involves reaching a conclusion or premise through the process of inquiry. The facts of a matter present themselves, but one must build conclusions through analyzing those facts and determining what they mean. Uncertainty about the conclusion at the beginning of the process of inquiry is the starting point. A very simple way to put it is to say that induction involves investigation. Is a given statement true? Inductive reasoning says, "Let's look at it more closely to determine what the statement actually says and then draw our conclusion."

Here is an example of inductive reasoning:

Question: Is Jesus the Son of God?

Process to discover if Jesus might be/is the Son of God:

1. Study the entire Bible to find any statements or proofs that would suggest or demonstrate that Jesus is the Son of God.
2. Study the Gospels to find any statements or proofs that would suggest or demonstrate that Jesus is the Son of God.
3. Study the Gospel of John to find any statements or proofs that would suggest or demonstrate that Jesus is the Son of God.
4. Study John 14 to find any statements or proofs that would suggest or demonstrate that Jesus is the Son of God.

In a modified inductive Bible study, the conclusions are not the starting point. Conclusions and summaries are derived from the science of hermeneutics (literature or language interpretation) or, to put it more simply, the scientific method consisting of observation, interpretation, and application. Students glean insights as they delve into the passage with the assistance of inquisitive questions. Any passage of the Bible is open to being handled through the modified inductive Bible study method, although it is granted that some passages are more easily handled than others. The modified emphasis is based on the assumption mentioned above that the teacher is the expert on the passage, has done the research, and provides some of the information that assists the process of induction. The teacher understands the purpose of the writing, the intended audience, the occasion for and date of the writing, and information about the author (if available), as well as themes and emphases in the book or passage. The teacher is both the group leader, as well as the premier student, who, due to preparation and previous study, understands the contextual questions, the meaning of the words, terms, etc. The inductive process is provided in partial fashion for the students; therefore, it is considered modified.

Other Considerations in Using the Modified Inductive Bible Study Method

Wrestling with the Text

The premise of the modified inductive Bible study method is that the students or learners do not accept the text or the passage at face value. The goal is to wrestle with the text in order to attempt to understand it more clearly and more deeply. The learners are to work hard at studying the words, phrases, and meaning of the text, analyzing it beyond any possible superficial meanings or impressions.

Questioning the Text

A modified inductive Bible study by necessity involves questioning the meaning of the text, i.e., asking question after question about the text or the selected passage that is being presented before the group. The leader and the group are not necessarily asking the higher critical questions that scholars like to ask, but questions that are willing to delve more deeply in order to get at meaning that might not be evident on the surface. This deeper meaning involves neither a mystical approach nor some sort of spiritualization of the text (as many wish to do, because it seems so cool). We are simply seeking to go beyond basic or surface knowledge and move toward true comprehension or understanding, as best we can determine it.

Discussion Creates Learning

The modified inductive Bible study method is built on the commitment—of the teacher or leader—to a pedagogical philosophy that group discussion among members is potentially as effective as the lecture method. As difficult as that commitment might be to believe—due to the commonality of didactic teaching experienced throughout most people's educational training—the leader must adhere to this basic assumption. On a personal level, I do indeed believe that more content can be passed along through the lecture/didactic approach, and I even love the dissemination of content and material. However, I still maintain that the discussions spawned by the modified inductive Bible study approach can resonate more deeply and impact the life of the learner more powerfully than the often frequently practiced method of rote learning. Lively discussions can cause the light bulbs to explode.

The Text (Subject) Is the Focus

When we deal with education, we must consider the three basic and essential factors of the learning triangle (figure 1, below):

1. The teacher
2. The student or learner
3. The subject

Viewed in a triangle, any of the three can function as the primary emphasis in the learning structure. The teacher can be the dominant factor in the process (such as the lecture method). The student can be the emphasis or focus in the learning process (such as hands-on experience initiated by the student—commonly called self learning or self instruction). Or, thirdly, the subject can take this role, so that the subject matter is the most important focus in the learning process.

In the triangle, there is a clear expectation that the learner will engage directly with the subject, along with the teacher, who is off to one side as a facilitator of sorts (in this case, an interpreter—not simply a facilitator). The learner is still beneath the teacher, as the teacher is able to structure the learning experience. The teacher teaches, trying to engage the student in the subject, i.e., the Scriptures or the biblical topic. Modified inductive bible study is what we might call content driven, i.e., we want the student to focus upon and be driven by the subject matter (the Scripture passage being considered).

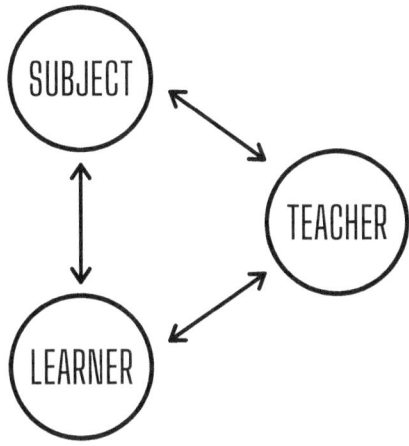

Figure 1: Subject/Learner/Teacher Paradigm[1]

The Learner as Active

In modified inductive Bible study, the learner is not passive but must be active and involved for the study to work. Such involvement is what brings the potential for constant dynamic and interaction into the group. Engagement with the text and with other learners brings an atmosphere of expectation and investigation. If the teacher/leader has the ability to stimulate and maintain multiple active learners, the study will be a success and exceptional learning will take place.

---

1. Atherton, "Learner, Subject and Teacher (3)."

Discovery

Another philosophical approach to learning in modified inductive Bible studies is the commitment of the teacher to promote and allow for discovery among the learners. In the lecture method of teaching, the discovery process is overwhelmingly to the benefit of the teacher, as she studies intensely in order to master the subject. The lecture method often plays out as simply as the teacher presenting her discoveries to passive students, who may or may not display light bulbs going off over the subject matter. In using the modified inductive Bible study method, the teacher is eager to involve the students in the process of personal inquisition and watch them well up with amazement at learning, comprehending, and applying some new truth. Inquiry leading to discovery is how the teacher facilitates the experience of light bulbs exploding.

The Teacher as Interpreter

As mentioned above, the teacher is a facilitator but not simply a facilitator. The teacher is an expert (or possibly, the expert!). He or she has completed much study and analysis and understands the passage well enough to teach it in a discourse or didactic (teaching/preaching) format. Hence, the teacher holds the most knowledge and uses—or interjects—it when necessary. He both leads and teaches. He may rebuke or correct when and where necessary. The teacher is more than a facilitator or guide of the discussion but has the information necessary to assure quality control over both the subject matter (material) and the free (but guided) discussion taking place in the modified inductive Bible study group context.

The Use of Questions in the Modified Inductive Bible Study Method[2]

The science of the modified inductive Bible study method deals with the skills to interpret and apply the respective passage. As mentioned above, the ability to question the text is imperative in order to properly and successfully facilitate the dynamic discussions. Asking questions of the text among a group of individuals is both a science and an art. I have discovered

---

2. McKenzie, "A Questioning Toolkit."

Lesson Planning: The Art of Asking Questions

that if the science isn't well understood, then the art plays out very poorly, leading to an ineffective small group experience.

The Essential Question

Growing up as a little child, I always dreaded our annual visits to the doctor's office. I wasn't sick that often, but there was always a required visit for a childhood disease shot or two, and I never had much willingness to confront those painful inoculations. Plus, the nurse was one of those authoritative autocrats who was short on the compassion aspect of bedside manner. She was efficient but not warmly so. I have memories that I cannot tell here, but they remain vivid six decades later. However, there was one enjoyable experience that made the trips to the doctor's office as a four- or five-year-old tolerable. That was found in the waiting room. There were a lot of magazines and other pieces of literature to be found on the end tables and magazine racks through which one could leaf while waiting for the call to enter the hallway to doom. And in that waiting room, I first experienced the pleasure of reading (or looking at) a children's magazine known as *Highlights*.

Highlights still exists, and I believe that even today the favorite activity of the magazine remains the feature that always fascinated me as a small child: Hidden Pictures. I think that everyone likes Hidden Pictures. The basic explanation is that the reader is presented with a very complicated or busily orchestrated picture—cartoonish in nature—with the challenge of finding a rather lengthy list of various unrelated items that one might discover in the picture if the onlooker is both diligent and persistent enough to keep delving. Hidden Pictures is a puzzle of sorts. And it is one of the most fun puzzles I have ever attempted to solve (I really don't like solving most puzzles). The primary requirements are to look earnestly, not give up, and pursue the answer that was presented in the list on the attendant page.

The modified inductive Bible study method is something like Hidden Pictures. The study leader must design inquisitive questions that will cause the learners to find those truths—or spiritual lessons—that are not readily apparent upon an initial reading of the respective text being studied. Diligence, inquiry, persistence, and serious pursuit of the original (and, hopefully, actual) meaning of the passage is necessary for the modified inductive Bible study to occur in a dynamic fashion. And the desire to create that dynamic of inquiry forces us to think through a very important dimension of the process, i.e., the nature and value of what is known as the essential question.

Therefore, it is necessary to begin by defining the concept revolving around the essential question. An essential question is a question that probes for deeper meaning and understanding of an issue, concept, or principle. The modified inductive Bible study will be best served if the leader understands the nature of essential questions and utilizes them in full capacity.

Essential questions fulfill the following purposes.

1. They set the stage for further questioning.
2. They foster the development of critical thinking skills.
3. They provoke deep thought.
4. They solicit information gathering and evaluation of data.
5. They result in original answers.
6. They make students produce original ideas rather than predetermined answers.
7. They may not have an answer.
8. They encourage critical thinking, not just memorization of facts.[3]

Example of the Essential Question and Its Development

An example of an essential question, for instance, might be individual health. Individual health is a concept (or essential question) out of which literally hundreds of other questions might derive. When you think of individual health (or your visit to the doctor), what are some of the deeper questions that come to mind?

1. How is the individual's general health? Is there a health problem with which to deal?
2. Does the individual have any untreatable health problems?
3. Does the individual regularly participate in unhealthy practices?

---

3. Atherton, "Learner, Subject and Teacher (3)."

Lesson Planning: The Art of Asking Questions

4. Are there hereditary factors that affect the individual's health? What are those factors? Can any of those hereditary factors be treated in any way?
5. Is weight a factor? What is causing weight problems? What practices can be prescribed to decrease (or increase, in some cases) weight gain?
6. Is fitness or lack of it a problem? Is the individual doing anything to enhance personal fitness? Does the individual exercise in any way? If so, what type of exercise? How often and for how long?
7. What are the individual's eating practices (and daily diet)?
8. What age is the individual? Is age a factor in affecting health?
9. Are there geographic factors influencing good or bad health?
10. Does the individual ever visit the doctor? Does the individual like, respect, dislike, or disrespect physicians? Does the individual participate in annual physical exams? Has the individual ever consulted with a health education professional?

As the reader can see, the process of asking questions regarding the essential question can become an endless endeavor. And the answers are all interesting, enlightening, and significant. An answer could easily lead to another set of questions. Eventually, these questions might lead to a conclusion or multiple conclusions.

This is the process involved in modified inductive Bible study, as the group observes the selected passage and makes inquiry into not only the statements in the passage but the meaning, intent, and application of the passage. As applied to the biblical text, the essential question asks about:

1. The author's intent
2. The theme or point of the text
3. The author's use of words and language
4. The implications and the applications of the text

The essential question as applied to the modified inductive Bible study method addresses the following basic hermeneutical (interpretive) questions:

1. Observation: What does the text say? Why is it worded the way it is?
- Word selection

- Phrases
- Connections

2. Interpretation: What does it mean (moving from knowledge to understanding)?

- Context and purpose of author
- Background and setting
- Compare and contrast
- Movement/flow/logic

3. Application: What does it mean to me/us/others (moving from knowledge to understanding to application)?

- General application and/or application to life and the world
- Personal application
- Assignment and accountability (are you going to follow through on your application?)

Essential Questions and Bloom's Taxonomy

Essential questions challenge students to think at the highest levels (or at least at higher levels) of Bloom's taxonomy by requiring critical evaluation and reflection. Bloom's taxonomy is a classification of learning objectives as applied to levels of learning in the educational and developmental process. As seen below in the pyramid chart (figure 2), Benjamin Bloom designated the following categories to describe the progress that the individual learner is making in the ability to understand and reason about information.

Breaking Down Bloom's Taxonomy in Simple Terms

Knowledge

At the bottom of the chart is the starting point or lowest level of education, i.e., the memorization of facts, terms, and basic concepts or knowledge (answering the question "What does it say?").

Understanding

The next level builds upon knowledge but goes beyond it by asking the question "What do the facts mean?" or "What is their significance?" This category is a much higher level known as *understanding* or *comprehension* (answering the question "What does it mean?").

Application

Building upon comprehension is the ability to move one's knowledge and understanding into working knowledge. The use of comprehended knowledge is *application* (answering the question "What does it mean to me and others?"). Application is a form of problem solving and truly brings relevance to the study of the text.

Analysis

Analysis involves taking the components of the information and examining them—or breaking them down—in parts or sections in order to see how the facts fit together or impact one another as a unit. The process of analysis certainly requires a higher level of thinking and involves integrative reasoning as well. Putting together the pieces of the puzzle brings both pleasure and joy to the discovery process in a modified inductive Bible study (answering the question "How does all this fit together?").

Synthesis

Synthesis is the next level of educational ability and involves putting together or combining the facts and concepts in order to build or construct smaller parts into a working whole or a larger reality. The best illustration I can provide for synthesis involves an early twentieth-century figure by the name of Howard Hughes. One day, when Hughes, one of America's early billionaires, was fourteen years old (in 1920), he entered the local auto dealership in his hometown and told the dealer that he wanted to buy the newest model of the Stutz Bearcat sports car and have it delivered to his home. Purchasing the expensive automobile was no problem since Howard's father was incredibly wealthy. But the dealer felt it necessary to call young Howard's father to see if it was really okay for him to sell the car at Howard's request. When speaking with Mr. Hughes, Howard's father asked, "What does he want to do with it?" Although Howard could (and would) drive the car, he told the dealer to tell his dad, "I want to take it apart and put it back together." His father then agreed that he could have the car, purchased it, and to his astonishment, watched Howard take it apart (*analysis*) and put it back together (*synthesis*). I think you would agree with me that such synthesis is a higher level of thinking and education. Synthesis is a challenge, and we will attempt to demonstrate it below (answering the question "How do we put the parts together to make a functional whole?").

Evaluation

Evaluation is the final stage of Bloom's taxonomy.[4] Evaluation entails looking at the entire process of the Bloom's taxonomy study and making judgments about the conclusions made or decisions derived as one works through that process. The learner attempts to question whether or not the knowledge, understanding, and application were appropriate, valuable, necessary, and/or good or bad (answering the question "Did we make the right decision based on the information we had and studied?").

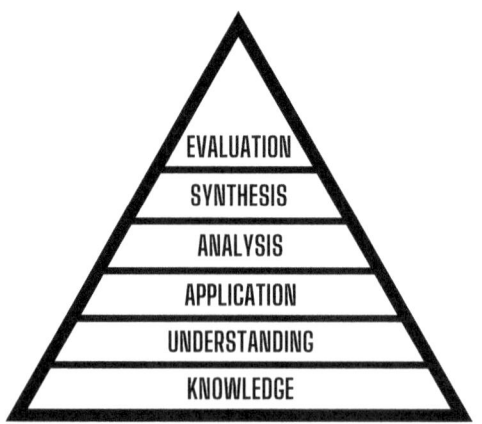

Figure 2: Bloom's Taxonomy

---

4. Interestingly, one of Dr. Bloom's former students, Lorin Anderson, did her own evaluation of Bloom's taxonomy, rearranging evaluation as the fifth level and putting synthesis at the top.

Lesson Planning: The Art of Asking Questions

Analyzing Bloom's Taxonomy

Two Examples

In order to demonstrate the use of Bloom's taxonomy for the purpose of developing vibrant discussion questions in a modified inductive Bible study, I am providing a brief explanation using two simple examples. A walk-through of the two examples will model the concepts inherent in Bloom's taxonomy. The explanation will begin with the bottom category of knowledge and end with the traditional final category of evaluation.

Knowledge: "Tell me what you see . . ."

Recall your knowledge. Knowledge deals with facts. Consider the following words: name, define, state, label, list, memorize, recall, order, recognize.

- The number two—two as a fact or concept; the number two could be a word or numeral without meaning (and it is a word or numeral without meaning up to a certain age. Just ask my two-year-old grandson how old he is. His answer is "toot," which doesn't address his age, but does have meaning!).
- Squirrel—this is a name for an animal, but if one has never seen the animal, this name is only a fact to be known.

Comprehension: "What do you understand?"

Explain your knowledge. Consider the following words: classify, describe, discuss, identify, recognize, select, translate.

- Two quarters can buy more than one quarter (comprehension of value).
- Squirrels are grey, frisky, little creatures with long tails, living and storing nuts in trees. (A chipmunk is not a squirrel; I have actually heard a child ask that question about a chipmunk. On April 4, 2014, I heard a small child—less than two years old—call a rooster a duck. Try that with the University of South Carolina and the University of Oregon! That is the difference between knowledge and comprehension.)

Application: "How can I apply this knowledge?"

Use your knowledge and comprehension. Consider the following words: apply, demonstrate, dramatize, employ, illustrate, interpret, operate, practice, solve, write.

- If I have two quarters and I add two quarters, I can shop at the dollar store (without tax).
- Squirrels are not pets. (Admittedly, chipmunks are not squirrels; nevertheless, for the sake of illustration, the following example will suffice: Using a detachable gutter—its go-to escape route—I once caught a chipmunk and placed it in a midsize aquarium with a screen top that we had purchased for previously owned hamsters. And while it sat in the container—for over an hour—it never moved. Needless to say, I was quite disappointed, as I was expecting all types of entertaining movement and activity. I gladly let it go, and cheerfully it went, back into the wild.)

Analysis: "What can you do if you compare this knowledge with other knowledge?"

Distinguish among the various aspects of your knowledge. Consider the following words: analyze, appraise, categorize, compare, contrast, criticize, differentiate, discriminate, examine, experiment, question, test. Words often used in analysis questions include analyze, why, take apart, diagram, draw conclusions, simplify, distinguish, and survey.

- Four coins that are quarters are more valuable than four coins that are nickels (do you remember when, as a child, someone explained to you that the small dime was more valuable than the bigger, heavier, and more appealing nickel? I do.)
- Squirrels are not as loyal as dogs and cats.

    Analysis—a few examples:

- "How does the size of a city affect the way people relate to each other?"
- "Why did the United States have a Civil War?"
- "What are some of the factors that cause heart attacks?"

Lesson Planning: The Art of Asking Questions

Synthesis: "What can I do or create if I put all of this knowledge together?"

Organize. Consider the following words: arrange, assemble, collect, compose, construct, create, design, develop, formulate, manage, plan, prepare, propose, set up, write.

- With my knowledge, comprehension, application, and analysis of coins and money values, I can run a cash register (or a bank).
- With my knowledge, comprehension, application, and analysis of various animals, I can write a book about animals as pets.

    Synthesis—a few examples:

- "How would you assemble these parts to construct a model airplane?"
- "How would your life be different if you never had to sleep?"
- "Put these Scrabble letters together to form a word on the board."

Evaluation: "What do I conclude, i.e., what is the value—what do I think—of the knowledge I have learned?"

Assess. Consider the following words: appraise, argue, compare, defend, estimate, judge, predict, rate, select, value. Words often used in evaluation questions include judge, rate, assess, evaluate. What is the best _____ in value?

- Running the cash register at McDonald's (or being the CEO at a national bank) would be fun (or lucrative)!
- Raising Doberman pinschers is more dangerous than raising toy poodles.

    Evaluation—a few examples:

- "What do you think about your work so far?"
- "Do you think that the pioneers did the right thing?"
- "Why do you think Benjamin Franklin is so famous?"

Walk-Through

Bloom's Taxonomy and Second Timothy 4:1–8

In order to apply the concepts found in Bloom's taxonomy, I am providing an example for the reader, drawing from the fourth chapter of Paul's second epistle to his son and fellow laborer in the gospel ministry, Timothy. I have provided questions for this passage based on each of Bloom's categories.

Second Timothy 4:1–8

I charge you in the presence of God and of Christ Jesus, who is to judge the living and the dead, and by his appearing and his kingdom: ²preach the word; be ready in season and out of season; reprove, rebuke, and exhort, with complete patience and teaching. ³For the time is coming when people will not endure sound teaching, but having itching ears they will accumulate for themselves teachers to suit their own passions, ⁴and will turn away from listening to the truth and wander off into myths. ⁵As for you, always be sober-minded, endure suffering, do the work of an evangelist, fulfill your ministry. ⁶For I am already being poured out as a drink offering, and the time of my departure has come. ⁷I have fought the good fight, I have finished the race, I have kept the faith. ⁸Henceforth there is laid up for me the crown of righteousness, which the Lord, the righteous judge, will award to me on that day, and not only to me but also to all who have loved his appearing.

Knowledge: "Tell me what you see . . ."

A. How are God and Christ Jesus described in verse 1?
B. What are some of the responsibilities and instructions Paul gives Timothy in verses 2 and 5?
C. How does Paul describe his life and ministry, which is now near its end, in verses 6 and 7?

Comprehension: "What do you understand?"

A. What is meant by Christ's judgment?

Lesson Planning: The Art of Asking Questions

    B. How does Christ's judgment (vv. 1, 8) affect Paul's view of life and ministry?

    C. Why does Paul value the preached word, according to verses 2–4?

    D. What does he mean by "a drink offering" and "his departure" in verse 6? (Note: the answers to these two concepts will require some study by the leader.)

Application: "How can I apply this knowledge?"

    A. How should Christ's judgment throne impact the Christian's (or my) life?

    B. In what ways have you seen Christians being poured out for the gospel like Paul describes?

    C. How is sound doctrine being attacked in the church today?

    D. How do I do the work of an evangelist?

Analysis: "What can you do if you compare this knowledge with other knowledge?"

    A. Compare a fight, a race, and a stewardship; how are they different (v. 7)?

    B. What is the difference between "being poured out like a drink offering" and a "departure?"

    C. What is the difference between the words correct, rebuke, and encourage?

Synthesis: "What can I do—or create—if I put all of this knowledge together?"

    A. If you started a church based on this text alone, what would it look like?

    B. If you used Paul's words in this text as a profile for hiring a pastor, what would he look like?

C. If you were giving a motivational speech (sermon) for living the Christian life based on this text, what would be your points?

Evaluation: "What do I conclude, i.e., what is the value—what do I think—of the knowledge I have learned?"

A. What do you think is Paul's most convincing or motivating statement in these verses?
B. What statement/verse do you think touched Timothy (his emotions) the most?
C. What statement/verse do you think impacted Timothy the most?

Considerations When Posing the Essential Question

Wait!

Give your students the time and opportunity to think through the possible answers and time to speak/answer before you tell them the answer. This consideration involves a lot of patience, some possible awkward moments, and sometimes a little prodding (or a restated question) if an answer is not forthcoming in a timely manner.

Engage Dialogue

Engage your students in dialogue and allow them to engage each other in dialogue. Be certain to build an atmosphere of discussion and interaction in a context of acceptance and disagreement. Also, allow them to ask questions of each other. But remember that you are more than a facilitator of guided discussion (just in case either opinions or discussions get out of hand).

Use Open-Ended Questions

Prompt student inquiry by asking them open-ended questions, i.e., questions that usually have no right answer. These are opinion questions. One of the primary reasons for using open-ended questions is that the participants

Lesson Planning: The Art of Asking Questions

tend not to answer the question that contains an obvious answer (or is a challenging higher-thought question).

Question to Avoid

As much as is possible, avoid yes and no questions. As a rule of thumb, do not use questions which can be answered yes or no. Normally, they go nowhere, i.e., they lead to little or no discussion. (If you do use a yes or no type of question, be sure to say, "Please explain or clarify your answer.")

Guide Discussion

Monitor the participants' progress in discussion and understanding, while guiding them with prompts or open-ended questions when necessary. Direct the discussion—and control it—when necessary. Remember (as mentioned above), you are the interpreter—not just a facilitator.

Some Cautions

The Use of Study Bibles

Please note, a good study Bible or a variety of study Bibles among the participants can kill a modified inductive Bible study. Instead of wrestling with the text or asking questions of the text and analyzing it, the participants will go into default mode, relying on the experts, and losing the dynamic of interaction and discovery. If necessary, provide the passage on a printout from a source that provides no notes (cross-references would be acceptable in this setting, however).

    I discovered this weakness a number of years ago when I was asked to lead a small group Bible study for a group of people who comprised the nucleus of a church plant in the greater Charlotte area. I was pretty excited about the possibility, since I had been involved so much in seminary administration and student ministry. Leading a local small group ministry of church laypeople appeared to be a great opportunity to be with and minister to everyday church members. And I decided, with great enthusiasm, that I would do a modified inductive Bible study using my beloved book of 1 John.

However, I did not anticipate the fact that this group of older, well-churched individuals would come to the Bible study with their own, well-marked, and thoroughly footnoted study Bibles. As I tried to engage the various members of this small group (there were ten or twelve of them) with basic questions dealing with the text of chapter 1 of 1 John, I discovered that their automatic default was to refer to the notes of their study Bibles, instead of trying to wrestle with the actual text of Scripture. Contrary to hearing their well-thought, or even weakly developed, answers, I kept hearing answers from John MacArthur, Charles Ryrie, and other Bible scholars.

Needless to say, the purpose of the small group modified inductive study—dynamic interaction and enlightened discussion—was completely thwarted. Honestly, I think that what they really wanted was a miniature sermon, and they would have been both ecstatic and content with a fifty-minute teaching time on my part. Sadly, although the group did meet together a couple more times, it dwindled itself into oblivion and never met together again. However, eventually this core group of people did start a church in the area, one that has been truly blessed over the years. The conclusion that I made from this experience was one that has left an indelible impression ever since: *study Bibles can kill Bible studies!* At least they have the potential to greatly diminish the effectiveness of modified inductive Bible studies.

Acknowledge Developmental Stages

The modified inductive Bible study can probably work to some extent with most any age group that is both able to read and interested enough to discuss the Bible and what it says. However, developmental stages are a factor in generating true interaction and discussion, including working through the higher levels of Bloom's taxonomy. It is my opinion that high school students, to some extent, would engage well in a modified inductive Bible study, college students would thrive on it, and most adults would be good candidates as well. However, at times, I have discovered that some adults have fallen into a mode of behavior or have personally developed strong convictions that prevent them from not appreciating the concept of wrestling with their beliefs, thinking deeply, or questioning the text. These adults will be frustrated by a modified inductive Bible study and frustrating to the leader of a modified inductive Bible study as well.

Conclusion

If you have read thus far in this work and persevered through some of the technical terminology, as well as the principles required in using and leading a modified inductive Bible study, you have certainly learned that there are a number of challenges in using this method of Bible study. The leader must indeed work, study, and contemplate (or think), as well as understand both the art and the science involved in this ministry of engaging Scripture. The leader must be willing to wrestle with the text, while simultaneously believing every word of it, and then convey her own enthusiasm over the truths that have been gained in her own personal study. The leader must develop good questions about the text. This is the toughest task, and some potential leaders might not be up to the demands required to meet the challenge. You must know your limits. The leader must also be able to assist the small group members in taking a fresh, new look at the particular passage, helping them to not only gain an accurate understanding (as much as is possible), but also engaging their emotions so that the meaning is impactful—additionally, Lord willing, showing them how to apply the text so that their own lives are changed by the Lord. The leader must pray, and prayer is work. The leader must ask God to be present in power, to use him or her as a leader, and to touch the lives of the members of the group so that they respond to his word. As the Holy Spirit works, the leader will watch the participants' understanding, emotions, and lives change, based upon the insights gleaned from the passage. Leading a modified inductive Bible study is challenging, but, believe me, the rewards are well worth the work. Wouldn't it be something for you to watch light bulbs exploding in the minds, hearts, and lives of God's children?

Appendix One

Disciple Investing through Modified Inductive Bible Study (MIBS)

Working through the Book of First John

First John
Modified Inductive Bible Study (MIBS)
Suggested Outline

Session	Topic	Passage
1	Introduction and Lesson One	1:1–4
2	Lesson Two	1:5–10
3	Lesson Three	2:1–6
4	Lesson Four	2:7–11
5	Lesson Five	2:12–17
6	Lesson Six	2:18–27
7	Lesson Seven	2:28—3:10

Appendix One

Session	Topic	Passage
8	Lesson Eight	3:11–18
9	Lesson Nine	4:1–6
10	Lesson Ten	4:7–12
11	Lesson Eleven	4:13–21
12	Lesson Twelve	5:1–5
13	Lesson Thirteen	5:6–12
14	Lesson Fourteen	5:13–21

Introduction and Lesson One

First John 1:1–4

Discussion Questions

NOTE TO LEADER

Answers to the questions below and suggestions for leading are provided for the leader, and those answers are in italics.

Fellowship and Introductions to One Another

Begin the small group study by building natural interaction among the participants and encouraging consistent attendance and involvement. There will be no homework or other assignments, but attending the Bible study and being involved in the discussion is crucial for the success of the group.

- Ask the following:
  - Name
  - Hometown
  - College major or present job

- Something unique about oneself that others might not know
- Talk about the need for attendance.
- Plan at least one social get-together for the first two or three months.

Leader opens in prayer.

NOTE TO LEADER

Once you get to know your participants better, you might feel comfortable asking one of them to open the study in prayer.

Introduction to First John

Hook for Initial Interest

For this first study, you want to provide some of the background of the book, e.g., authorship, recipients, purpose(s) of the book, key themes, etc. You are already teaching the participants some principles of interpretation (or hermeneutics).

Question

If you were to buy a new or used car, what types of things would you consider before signing your life away?

NOTE TO LEADER

You have full liberty to make up your own questions at any point. These questions are provided in order to guide you in the science of the modified inductive Bible study method.

POSSIBLE ANSWERS

Age, mileage, tires, engine, make, ownership, previous damage, previous owners, color, wear and tear, etc.

Appendix One

Book (Background)

Facts about First John

- **Author:** John, the apostle. Note the parallel passages (and you might take the time to look at these with the group).
    - *He is an eyewitness of Christ*—1:3 (context: 1:1–3):
      Cf. John 21:24: "This is the disciple who is bearing witness about these things, and who has written these things, and we know that his testimony is true."
    - *Keeping commands proves love*—2:3:
      Cf. John 14:21: "Whoever has my commandments and keeps them, he it is who loves me. And he who loves me will be loved by my Father, and I will love him and manifest myself to him."
    - *John is the loving disciple*—3:1:
      Cf. John 21:7a: "That disciple whom Jesus loved therefore said to Peter, 'It is the Lord!'" (The word *love* is used twenty-one times in 1 John 4 alone.)
    - *Love is proven by laying down your life*—3:16:
      Cf. John 15:13: "Greater love has no one than this, that someone lay down his life for his friends."
- **Date:** AD 90–95 (late in the first century)—time for heresies to develop (*think of how gossip/rumors spread in time*).
- **Recipients:**
    - 2:1, 18a: A group he knows and affectionately loves (in Asia Minor)
    - 2:28: Christians in general (1 John is considered to be what is called a general or universal letter to all Christians everywhere)
- **Purpose:**
    - To warn Christians about false teachings and philosophies (4:1)
    - To give them a certainty of what they believe (1:1–4; 5:12–13—*these are considered to be the key—or summary—verses of the book*)
    - To encourage them to love (4:7ff)
- **Themes (apply to both new Christians and unsure Christians):**

- Proofs of salvation:
  - 2:9: Love *(the social test: how do you love?)*
  - 2:29: Righteousness *(the moral test: how do you live?)*
  - 2:22–23: Doctrine—Truth *(the doctrinal test: what do you believe?)*
- Assurance of salvation (5:12–13)
- Fruit (righteousness) comes from true salvation (2:3–6)

- **Problem:** Gnosticism (These false teachers separated matter and spirit: *matter and flesh are evil, while spirit is good, so it is okay to sin in the flesh, because that doesn't affect one's spirit.*)
- **General Application Question:** How is gnosticism seen or exhibited in today's world?
  - Two types of gnosticism:
    - Docetism *(deals with truth—seems true)*: God can't be known; Christ didn't really live in his body; it just seemed that way. God can't die (his spirit came upon Jesus at baptism and departed prior to his death on the cross).
    - Cerinthianism *(deals with righteousness)*: emphasizing pleasure and licentiousness (freedom of the flesh), Cerinthianism demonstrated a libertine spirit: the flesh is evil, but it doesn't matter what the flesh does, as long as the spirit is right. (However, John combats this teaching by emphasizing that Christ was God who actually took upon himself human flesh, i.e., the incarnation did not make Jesus sinful.)

Lesson One

Now that we have considered the introductory material regarding the book of 1 John, we turn our attention to the text, 1 John 1:1–4, using the modified inductive Bible study method.

- **Verse 1:** "That which was from the beginning, which we have heard, which we have seen with our eyes, which we looked upon and have touched with our hands, concerning the word of life . . ."
  - What could be meant by the word *beginning*?

Appendix One

Eternal Christ; cf. beginning/Word with God; cf. John 1:1–2, 14

- What is John trying to prove in these first two to three verses of chapter 1?
- Do you see a progression of experience in verse 1? What is it? Describe it.
- What is the difference between seen and looked upon?
  Looked upon means to grasp the significance—goes beyond just seeing.
- What are the three higher senses of humans that are mentioned here?
  - *Hearing*
  - *Sight*
  - *Touch*
- How does this relate to the false teaching that John was addressing?
  Gnostics (he seemed) → No, he is a material reality.

- **Verse 2:** ". . . the life was made manifest, and we have seen it, and testify to it and proclaim to you the eternal life, which was with the Father and was made manifest to us . . ."

  - What is the result of seeing the manifested Christ? How do we see Christ today? *(Cf. 1 Pet 1:8—"Though you have not seen him, you love him. Though you do not now see him, you believe in him and rejoice with joy that is inexpressible . . ." The answer is that we see and know Christ by faith and through the Scriptures that reveal him to us.)*
  - What do you think is the difference between the concepts/words bear witness/testify and the word proclaim?
    - *Testify: personal experience; proclaim: pass it on*
    - *Note the progression: seen → testify/personal experience → pass on*
  - What is the relationship between knowing Christ and telling others about him?

- **Verse 3:** ". . . that which we have seen and heard we proclaim also to you, so that you too may have fellowship with us; and indeed our fellowship is with the Father and with his Son Jesus Christ."

- Define Christian fellowship.
- Why might these readers not have had fellowship with John?
- What causes a break in Christian fellowship?
  - *Relational differences—personality*
  - *Doctrinal differences or disagreements (1 John)*
  - How do you correct problems in these areas?
- How is fellowship different from friendship?
- What does it mean to fellowship with the Father and the Son? How does this happen?

Possible Answers

Quiet times/personal devotions—prayer by faith

Personal Application

Fellowship with all Christians is a demonstration of our unity in Christ, yet difficult with those who are difficult to love. How do we love the unlovely or those to whom we are not drawn naturally?

- **Verse 4:** "And we are writing these things so that our joy may be complete."
  - "our joy"—why this phrase?
    Fellowship creates unity/joy.
  - How does fellowship create joy?
    - *The readers can have true fellowship with God.*
    - *The writers will receive joy from the disciples who are walking with God.*
  - How does loss of fellowship create loss of joy?
  - Why might they lose fellowship with these believers?
    The effect of sin and heresy from the false teachers will divide them.

Lesson Two

First John 1:5–10

Discussion Questions

Hook(s)

Question 1

If a person says that he is a Christian (a believer), but you know that he is living a life that is obviously sinful (i.e., immoral), how would you approach him in trying to get him to understand that he is wrong (or to get him to recognize his condition or to return to the Lord)?

Question 2 (optional)

What are some examples of personal denial that we see today? What types of denial have you seen? Why do people fall into denial or patterns of denial?

- **Verse 5:** "This is the message we have heard from him and proclaim to you, that God is light, and in him is no darkness at all."
    - Why would John write that his message is "God is light" rather than "God is love" or "Christ died for you" or something else? What point might he be making?
        - *Knowing we are in the faith begins with our understanding of God.*
        - *John is trying to emphasize the purity of God and how it must impact the purity of God's followers.*
    - What do you think of when you think of light (i.e., attributes of light)?

Working through the Book of First John

Possible Answers

Revealing (truth), pure (righteousness), warm (love) (cf. the three themes of 1 John)

- no darkness—when describing God, what does that mean?
  No sin, no falsehood (impurity); no lack of understanding

- **Verse 6:** "If we say we have fellowship with him while we walk in darkness, we lie and do not practice the truth."
  - Here John is addressing the heretical problems facing these believers. What were those problems? Can anyone remember?
    - *Gnosticism*
      1. *These false teachers separated matter/spirit: matter and flesh are evil, while spirit is good, so it is okay to sin in the flesh, because that doesn't affect one's spirit.*
      2. *It only seemed that Christ came in the flesh.*
  - What do you think are the requirements for true Christian fellowship?

Possible Answers

- *Openness/transparency toward God and one another—truth*
- *Love for and obedience to God—love*
- *Verbal relationship—the will to relate honestly—righteousness*

- *Point:* John can be very black and white about sin. You're either one (in the light) or the other (in darkness). You either lie, or you are in the truth.
  - Fellowship with light (truth) ≠ walking in darkness ∴ sin is important

Personal Application

How does sin hinder our fellowship with God?

- What does the word *walk* signify about the Christian life?
  Habit and practice (continuance)—moving step by step in a forward direction

Appendix One

Personal Application

What are areas of darkness here (in our city, community, neighborhood, apartment complex, on our campus, on the military base, in your work place, etc.) that will prevent your fellowship (i.e., as a Christian) with the Father?

- *Technology addiction, sports, lust, or easy access to pornography, parties with too much drinking, dorm life, peer pressure, staying out of the word and prayer, wasting time, too much television or media absorption, etc.*
- How can/will we overcome these temptations?

- **Verse 7:** "But if we walk in the light, as he is in the light, we have fellowship with one another, and the blood of Jesus his Son cleanses us from all sin."
  - This is a conditional statement: "if we walk in the light as he himself is in the light"
    - What does walking in the light mean?
      Walking in revelation—the light of Christ and God's word; being obedient to God's revealed will
    - Why does he say "if"? (Does this demand perfection? Why or why not?)
    - How do believers step out of walking in the light?
  - What is the promise of the conditional statement?
    - We will have fellowship with one another.
    - The blood of Jesus cleanses from all sin.
  - If we are already Christians and walking in the light, why do we need the blood of Jesus to cleanse us?
    Because we still sin and need forgiveness on a daily basis, believing the gospel every day
  - How does blood cleanse us of sin?
    You may need to carry on a discussion regarding the Old Testament sacrificial system (cf. Lev 16:15–22; Heb 9:11ff, esp. vv. 22–23).
  - How does this cleansing blood give us assurance?
- **Verse 8:** "If we say we have no sin, we deceive ourselves, and the truth is not in us."

- How is verse 8 a logical consequence of verses 5, 6, and 7?
- Why would someone claim to be without sin (i.e., deny his sin)? *He dooesn't want to admit that he still sins or falls out of walking in the light—feels guilt, shame, or unacceptable to others. He might be afraid of losing his salvation.*
  - If the group is knowledgeable enough, feel free to discuss Christian traditions that deny daily, personal sin, i.e., perfectionism, Wesleyan Methodism, and Pentecostal holiness traditions, etc.
  - Explain the difference between daily righteousness (walking in the light and avoiding sin) and positional righteousness (i.e., I, as a believer in Christ, am always accepted before God because of the righteousness of Christ).
  - *Remember and reflect upon the background (purpose of the book): gnostics believed it was permissible to sin in the flesh, as long as the spirit was okay.*
- Where do we find biblical proof for the fact that we all sin and are sinful?
  - *Cf. Gen 3–4—the fall of Adam and Eve leads to an inherited sin nature that results in the murder of Abel by Cain.*
    (*Note:* the entire Bible rests on this account!)
  - *See Rom 3:9–20 and Rom 5:6–21.*
    (*Note:* both of these passages are lengthy studies in themselves. Do not spend an inordinate amount of time dwelling on them here.)
- Do you feel that people in the West generally believe that they are sinful, or is this a lost concept? Why?
- How do people today define sin?
- Why would we prefer or choose to deceive ourselves (or rationalize our sin), when it means that we are actually sinning by telling others we have no sin?
  We don't want to . . .
  - *Face responsibility and/or the need for restoration*
  - *Admit personal failure*

- *Embarrass ourselves before others*
- *Obey God*
- *Apologize for our wrongs*
- *Face God's rebuke or chastisement, because of the fear of the consequences or the need to change and repent*

- **Verse 9:** "If we confess our sins, he is faithful and just to forgive us our sins and to cleanse us from all unrighteousness."
  - What does it mean to confess our sins?
    - *To be honest about our moral failures before God*
    - *To repent of specific sins that we have committed*
  - Why is confession necessary?
  - How is confession related to the denial of our sins mentioned in verse 8 above ("If we say we have no sin, we deceive ourselves, and the truth is not in us")?
  - How or why would God be faithful to forgive us (if we confess our sins)?
  - Why would God be just to forgive us of our sins?
  - If we are already forgiven by God as believers in Christ, why do we need assurance of forgiveness? How is confession of our sins related to forgiveness?
    - *Our daily walk includes the commission of specific sins that, if known in our hearts and minds, must be repented of in order to maintain fellowship with God and not grieve the Holy Spirit.*
  - Why is assurance that we are purified from all unrighteousness important? How would you live/feel if you could not live with assurance of forgiveness of your sins?

- **Verse 10:** "If we say we have not sinned, we make him a liar, and his word is not in us."
  - What two things in this verse does denying our sin say about God?
  - How does denying our personal sin demonstrate our lack of understanding of God?
  - What does God's word say or teach about sin and sinners?

- How does verse 10 relate to the gnostic heresy that we previously considered?
  - *The false teachers ignored sins of the flesh and justified them as long as the spirit wasn't being negatively affected.*

Lesson Three

First John 2:1–6

Discussion Questions

Hook

What are some of the reasons people will call a lawyer? At what point of trouble does a person consider calling a lawyer? Do you have any examples? (*Note: keep this short—a discussion of this nature could go on forever.*)

Introduction

- Can you recall the three themes (proofs of salvation) of the book of 1 John?
  1. *Social (love—how are you doing in your love for others?)*
  2. *Moral (righteousness—how are you living? Are you holy?)*
  3. *Doctrinal (truth—what do you believe about Christ?)*
- **Read 1 John 2:1–6.**
  - With which theme does 1 John 2:1–6 deal? *Moral*
- **Review:** Look at chapter 1—read (skim) briefly.
  - What do you think John's main theme or point is thus far?
  - How is he presenting his argument—i.e., how is he relating the theme to the readers, getting them to think? What does he say about false teaching and the truth of God? What is the main point of 1 John 1:5–10?
    - *False teaching = I am without sin (vv. 8, 10)*

- *True teaching = you are sinful* (he has concluded in 1:5–10 that Christians do sin!)

Assignment

Read 1 John 2:1–6 once more. This time while reading, circle, underline, or note the words that are frequently used or repeated.

Note to Leader

Outline for vv. 1–2: remedy for sin; vv. 3–6: proof that remedy was taken

- *Words*
  - *Sin—v. 1 (x2), v. 2 (x2)*
  - *Know—vv. 3, 4, 5*
- *Expressions*
  - *Commandment—vv. 3, 4*
  - *In him—vv. 4, 5 (x2), 6*

- **Verse 1:** "My little children, I am writing these things to you so that you may not sin. But if anyone does sin, we have an advocate with the Father, Jesus Christ the righteous."
  - "My little children"—Who is the author? For what is he known? *He is the disciple whom Jesus loved. He is known as a loving disciple, the one who knows intimate love; the aged apostle.*
  - Why does he call these believers "my little children"?
    - *He is expressing fatherly affection.*
    - *He also is the aged apostle.*
  - What else is he saying about these believers and his relationship with them?

  Personal Application

  He has adopted them as his own. Whom have you loved in such a way that they feel adopted by you?

  - What are "these things" he mentions in 2:1?

Appendix One

- How does 2:1 (the purpose of the letter) relate to 1:5–10, i.e., "not to sin"?
  He has concluded in 1:5–10 that Christians do sin, but he is not encouraging them to actually sin with intent.
- If someone authoritatively told us that God expects us to sin, what might our natural response be?
- How does our culture define sin?
  - *Making mistakes*
  - *Not being perfect*
  - *False guilt*
  - *Hurting others*
  - *Doing something wrong*
  - *Committing a serious crime*
  - *Being a bad person (worse than me)*
- How does the Bible define sin?
  - *Trespass—commission (rebellion against God and his will)*
  - *Falling short—omission (failure to obey God's commands)*
  - *Unbelief—not willing to trust in or believe God and his promises*
- What are our natural responses to our sins?
  - *Guilt, shame, hiding, rationalizing*
- Do you ever get concerned (or worry) about your sin? Why or why not?
- Should Christians emphasize sin? Do we over- or underemphasize it?
- If you broke the law and were caught and taken to jail, what would you do?
  - *Call a lawyer?*
  - *What considerations would you make in hiring a lawyer?*
- Why is Jesus characterized as the righteous?
  - *He has no record of lawbreaking.*
  - *He is perfect in every way.*

- ◆ *He can present his case without flaw.*
- **Verse 2:** "He is the propitiation for our sins, and not for ours only but also for the sins of the whole world."
  - What is an atoning sacrifice (or propitiation)?
    A means of getting into right relationship with God through the use of a sacrificial system ordained by God himself. As our advocate, Jesus obtains mercy for us before the judging eye of a perfect and holy God.
    - ◆ *Cf. Num 5:5–8; Isa 53:4–7.*
  - What does he mean by the phrase "the whole world"?
    1. *Us = believers; whole world = unbelievers*
    2. *Us = Jews; whole world = Gentiles, in addition to the nation of Israel*
  - Does "the whole world" mean that everyone is now forgiven because of Christ's work? Explain.

  PERSONAL APPLICATION
  - ◆ In your daily life, what type of people do you tend to avoid (if you are willing to answer this question; it can be awkward)?
  - ◆ How does this verse help us overcome our prejudices or discomfort with others who are not like us?
  - ◆ *Application point*: God is not a respecter of persons but loves the whole world, every individual ever conceived.
- **Verse 3:** "And by this we know that we have come to know him, if we keep his commandments."
  - Is John being legalistic in this verse? *(legalism—trying to please or appease God in action but not in heart)*
    - ◆ What does "keep" mean?
      Observe, guard, watch, pay attention to, obey
    - ◆ Does obeying save us? Then why obey (what is the motivation for obedience)?
      Gratitude, joy, peace, reward (i.e., good consequences; obedience brings blessing; cf. John 14:21)

Appendix One

Personal Application

How do our culture's rules/commandments relate to God's? Must we keep these and other rules of man/government? Why or why not?

- **Verse 4:** "Whoever says 'I know him' but does not keep his commandments is a liar, and the truth is not in him . . ."
  - Why such an emphasis on God's commandments? How is the gnostic heresy addressed by this verse?
    - *Profession of belief is not legitimate if one practices the freedom of the flesh (sensualism).*
    - *The gnostics did not think sinning in the body affected one's standing before God. The spirit was important (belief), but the flesh did not impact the spirit.*
  - How do we see gnosticism in the church/world today?
    - *Christians defending premarital sex, as long as you still love God*
    - *Christians justifying moral disobedience, because they are spiritual in other things (church attendance, reading their Bibles, praying, doing acts of mercy, etc.)*
  - If Jesus rebuked the Pharisees for keeping 613 manmade laws (based on the Ten Commandments), why should we try to keep God's law? (What was the problem?)
    - *They didn't have a heart for God.*
    - *They kept the commandments in order to work their way to God.*
    - *They were interested in showing others how good they were (in external obedience). They were men pleasers.*
    - *We should obey God because we love him and want to please him, based on Christ's work on the cross on our behalf. We are not trying to prove to others how good we are.*
  - In what ways does obeying and following God's law impact or affect the believer?
    - *As a guide for the believer*
    - *As an inspiration to do the will of God*

- How is the believer enabled to obey and follow God's law?
  - *Through the power of the Holy Spirit based on understanding the gospel*
  - *By God's grace and help*
- Why does John mention two statements, i.e., why does he say what appears to be the same thing twice? 1) "He is a liar." 2) "The truth is not in him."
  - Which of the two statements do you think is the more grievous accusation? Why?

Possible Answer

The harsher statement is the one that reflects the bigger problem—the inner man.

- **Verse 5:** ". . . but whoever keeps his word, in him truly the love of God is perfected. By this we may know that we are in him . . ."
  - Why the change to his word rather than saying commands? What is the difference between the two?
    His word is more comprehensive. Commands are simply part of his word.
  - How does obedience prove love?
    - (*Cf. John 14:21:* "Whoever has my commandments and keeps them, he it is who loves me. And he who loves me will be loved by my Father, and I will love him and manifest myself to him.")
  - Give an example of obedience being done without love.
    - *Military settings—soldiers to their commanding officers*
    - *Police officers—civilians doing what they are required to do*
    - *Bosses—obeying in order to keep your job or position*
    - *Parents—obeying out of fear or duty*
- **Verse 6:** ". . . whoever says he abides in him ought to walk in the same way in which he walked."

Appendix One

Note to Leader

This is the remedy for evaluating the moral test, although you know that you will sin.

- What does it mean to live as Jesus did?
  - *To walk in love, love for God the Father and love for others*
  - *To walk in purity, seeking holiness*
  - *To walk, led by the Spirit*
  - *To walk in obedience to the Father's will*
  - *To walk in humility and as a servant*
  - Others?
- Does God expect us to be perfect (as Jesus) or simply just to do our best? What does our best look like?

Application

- How did Christ walk in relation to others? Are there illustrations of which you can think?
- What are the problems in your present situation that tempt or cause you to live selfishly and not like Jesus?

Lesson Four

First John 2:7–11

Discussion Questions

Hook

If you were trying to select the one characteristic of a Christian's life that should stand out the most in proving that person to be a Christian, what would it be?

Possible Answers

Humility, love, kindness, patience, joy, honesty, obedience, faith/belief, conviction, wisdom, peace, justice, mercy, forgiveness, etc.

Possible follow-up question:

Out of all of the answers just cited, can we come to an agreement on one answer?

Note to Leader

This question allows for greater discussion and thoughtful prioritizing, but could use up too much time.
- Recall the three themes (tests of assurance or salvation) of the book: truth (doctrinal), righteousness (moral), love (social).
    - Which of these three would you say is most lacking in Christians today?

Appendix One

- **Verse 7:** "Beloved, I am writing you no new commandment, but an old commandment that you had from the beginning. The old commandment is the word that you have heard."
- **Context**: In verses 3–6, how do we know if a person truly knows God?
  - *Keeps God's commands*
  - *Obeys God's word*
  - *Walks like Jesus walked*
  - What should be our primary motivation for keeping God's commandments?
    Love for God (through the Spirit of God); gratitude; gospel understanding; adoption
  - What are some *false* motivations?
    Fear (God will get you); legalism; guilt; pleasing others; pride; self-righteousness; showing off like the Pharisees
  - Notice that John says, "I am writing you no new command . . ."
    - Do you see any hint of a command in the previous verses?
      Verse 6—to walk in love is to walk as Christ walked (vv. 9–11 = love)
  - What does "from the beginning" mean?

  Possible answers
  1. *Christ coming to and living on earth (cf. 1 John 1:1)*
  2. *These believers' conversions*
  3. *The Old Testament commands, especially*

  - What do you think is the old command or message they had heard?

  Possible Answers
  - *See John 13:34–35: "A new commandment I give to you, that you love one another: just as I have loved you, you also are to love one another.* [35] *By this all people will know that you are my disciples, if you have love for one another."*

- *See Matt 22:37–38: Jesus defines the two greatest commandments—love the Lord with all your heart, etc., and love your neighbor as yourself.*

Personal Application

- How does/did your life change when you experience/experienced the love of Christ personally?
- How can we share Christ's love with others?
  Reaching out to new people and people we don't know; finding avenues of ministry to others; taking care of others' needs.

- **Verse 8:** "At the same time, it is a new commandment that I am writing to you, which is true in him and in you, because the darkness is passing away and the true light is already shining."
  - Why is the command called new?
    It is new because . . .
    - *Its truth is seen in him—Deut 6:5 (the old—"Love the LORD your God with all your heart and with all your soul and with all your strength"). How is it seen in him?—Deut 6:5 is fulfilled by Christ—he fulfills the law completely.*
    - *Its truth is seen in you—these believers are experiencing this love for the first time.*
  - What does "the darkness is passing away" mean?

Possible Answers

- *The rule of Satan is now being conquered by the victory of the cross.*
- *The gospel is going forth to the nations.*
- *Believers are lights of Christ all over the place.*

Appendix One

Personal Application:

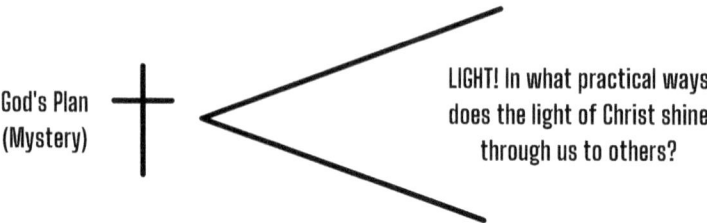

Figure 3: From Mystery to the Light of Christ (1 John 2:9)

- **Verse 9:** "Whoever says he is in the light and hates his brother is still in darkness."
    - How would you define hate?
    Animosity, lack of love, resentment, evil, revenge, extreme dislike, abhorrence, hostility
    - How is hate expressed?
    Prejudice, envy, jealously, anger, rejection, arrogance, division, personal attacks, death threats, racial division, racism, etc.
    - How does hate begin in our hearts?

    Possible answers

    Motivated by misjudging, selfishness, insecurity, fear, judgmentalism, lack of compassion
    - How have you seen this hypocrisy (i.e., someone says, "I am in the light," but the person actually hates others)?
- **Verse 10:** "Whoever loves his brother abides in the light, and in him there is no cause for stumbling."
    - What does "no cause of stumbling" mean?

    Possible Answers

    Avoids sinning against another or does not cause himself to fall into a mentality of hatred (the context: hatred).
    - Application: How do we cause ourselves to fall/stumble into hatred?

- How does love keep us from stumbling?
- How do we cause others to stumble?

PossIBLE ANSWERS

We gossip or slander; we criticize; we attack others verbally; we polarize our opinions for effect.

- **Verse 11:** "But whoever hates his brother is in the darkness and walks in the darkness, and does not know where he is going, because the darkness has blinded his eyes."
  - Why is hatred defined as being "in the darkness" and "walking in the darkness"?

  PossIBLE ANSWERS:
  - *God's love is light.*
  - *They have no fellowship with God.*
  - *Darkness is the domain of evil.*
  - *Hatred destroys.*

  - What does it mean to be spiritually blind?
  - Why are people who hate others described as not knowing where they are going?

  PossIBLE ANSWERS
  - *They aren't following God's will.*
  - *They are blind to their evil and its consequences as it affects others (this is the darkness).*
  - *The path without love is destructive and a dead end.*

  - What keeps/prevents us from reaching out to others in love?
  - What is Christ doing in your life now that would motivate you to reach out to and/or share life with others?
  - In what ways is the hater described?
    - *Present state ("is in" and "walks in" the darkness)—out of fellowship with God*

- *Present action—walking, i.e., living as the world*
- *Future (goal)—no certainty of his or her end (cannot claim to be a Christian, going to heaven)*
- *Blinded—not just a hindrance, but destruction*
  - Application: How do those living in darkness feel about Jesus/the Bible/spiritual things?

Final Exercise (optional)

Note to Leader

There may not be time for this discussion.

- Reread 1:1—2:11 and note the character of the Christian versus the character of the non-Christian.

Lesson Five

First John 2:12–17

Discussion Questions

Hook

What would you say is a sign of Christian maturity?—i.e., at what point of your Christian life do you know you are reaching or have reached maturity? How do you know?

POSSIBLE ANSWERS

Spiritually discerning, prayer life, victory over nagging sins, others-focused, servant attitude, able to encourage others, knowledge of Scripture, trusting God—less worry, prayer for and love for your enemies, patience in all circumstances

Context

What is the thrust of verses 9–11? How would these verses affect the honest (young) believer?

POSSIBLE ANSWER

Guilt over not being loving enough or harboring bad attitudes toward others, resentment

Appendix One

Lesson Five

Stages of Maturity

Verses 12–14: These verses are descriptions of Christians in various stages of growth, based upon chronological and/or age categories of maturity.

- Why does John designate these three groups? How might they connote levels of maturity?
- Remember these basic interpretation guidelines:
    - What does it say?
    - What does it mean?
    - What does it mean to me?
- **Verse 12:** "I am writing to you, little children, because your sins are forgiven for his name's sake."
    - This is an introduction to all believers/recipients of the letter—recall the purpose of writing for the book (cf. 1:4, 2:1).
    - "little children"—What would this expression signify to those who read/hear it?

    POSSIBLE ANSWERS

    - *It is a term of endearment—John is like a father to the readers.*
    - *They are new or young (in faith) believers.*

    - How are the little children described in verses 12–14?
        - *Those who are forgiven—cf. 1:9; 2:1–2*
        - *Those who have the Father*
    - What is the meaning of "forgiven for his name's sake"?
    The name represents:
        - *Who he is (Messiah and Lamb of God)*
        - *What he has done (a sacrifice for his people's sins)*
        - *The authority of forgiveness*
- **Verses 13–14:** "I am writing to you, fathers, because you know him who is from the beginning. I am writing to you, young men, because you have overcome the evil one. I write to you, children, because you

know the Father. ¹⁴I write to you, fathers, because you know him who is from the beginning. I write to you, young men, because you are strong, and the word of God abides in you, and you have overcome the evil one."

- Study each group: Why is each its own category, i.e., what is distinctive about each group?
  - Children (v. 14)—"you know the Father"—beginning intimacy with God, who is a father to them

  PERSONAL APPLICATION

  Making time to spend with God in personal devotion(s) so that you might continue to know him

  - Young men
    - "You have overcome the evil one"

      PERSONAL APPLICATION

      How do young, growing believers get tempted and tested, and how do they overcome Satan (cf. 1 Peter 2:11)?

      - How is a new/young believer's temptation different from a maturing believer's temptation? Is there a difference?
      - What are the positive results of overcoming Satan and sin in the life of a believer?
    - "You are strong"
      - How does enduring and overcoming temptation strengthen believers?

      PERSONAL APPLICATION

      How did Jesus conquer his temptations (cf. Luke 4:1ff)?
    - "The word of God abides in you"
      - How do you think that the word of God was abiding in these growing Christians?

Appendix One

Personal Application

How do we learn to let the word of God abide in us?

- *Spending time in the word of God*
- *Scripture memory*
- *Living wholly by biblical standards*
- *Integrating faith in the Word into daily life*

- Fathers—"You know him who has been from the beginning"
  - What is the difference between the concepts knowing him, i.e., God (addressed to little children), and knowing him who is from the beginning (addressed to fathers)?

Possible Answers

- *The children have an introductory knowledge and relationship with God, and the fathers are those with a deeper knowledge of the eternal God.*
- *The fathers understand something about Jesus's deity (his eternal nature—John 1:1) and have persevered (a sign of maturity) through the false teaching that threatens these believers (cf. 1:1–3).*

Admonitions to All the Children

- **Verse 15:** "Do not love the world or the things in the world. If anyone loves the world, the love of the Father is not in him."
  - What is meant by the word *world*?
    - *No love for the world—the system of belief that rebels against God; in this sense, it is ruined and depraved.*
    - *The original Greek for "do not love" means "stop what is now in progress."*

Personal Applicatio:

What does it mean to love the world? How is love for the world expressed in our or others' lives?

- What is the difference between the world and the things (literally, "that") in the world?
  - *The world is a general term for the principles of unbelief and the things of the world that would be specific temptations or dangers (which will be listed by John below)*
  - *No love for the things in the world—that which might cause us to be hostile or indifferent to God, as we are enamored of them*

Personal Application

What are the things in the world that we tend to love over God? Why do things gain our affection so easily?

Description of the World

Note to Leader

You will find these same desires/temptations described in both Christ's battle with Satan in the wilderness, which ended in complete victory (cf. Matt 4:1–11), and Adam and Eve's confrontation with Satan, which ended in utter sin and failure (cf. Gen 3:1–6). To take time to look at these passages would bring great insight to these verses in 1 John 2:15–17, but would also most probably make this lesson into two separate lessons.

- **Verse 16:** "For all that is in the world—the desires of the flesh and the desires of the eyes and pride of life—is not from the Father but is from the world."
  - Describe these three attributes/areas of this world that are against God.
    - *Lust/desires of the flesh—sensualism: doing—eating, drinking, sex, drugs, pleasure recreation, hedonism, pornography, idolatries in anything sensual, wasting time, self-gratification, etc.*
    - *Lust/desires of the eyes—materialism: having—ownership, technology, cars, clothes, house(s), possessions, whatever else we prioritize to have for ourselves*
    - *Pride of life—egoism: being—acceptance, status, prominence, intellect, conceit, vanity, arrogance, lust for honor and esteem, craving for attention*

Appendix One

- What would be the opposite of these three attitudes?

Possible Answers

- *Self-control, self-discipline, restraint, purity, modesty*
- *Contentment, gratitude, sacrifice, simplicity in living*
- *Humility, understanding one's identity in Christ, servanthood, submission, meekness, lowliness*

Personal Application

How do we develop the traits above as Christians?

- **Verse 17:** "And the world is passing away along with its desires, but whoever does the will of God abides forever."
  - How does John describe the world in verses 16 and 17?
    - *Not of the Father*
    - *Is presently passing away with its lusts; therefore, it is always approaching judgment*
  - How does John describe believers?
    - *They do the will of God.*
    - *They abide/remain forever—for eternity (see context, vv. 18–19).*

Personal Application

How do the answers in the question above impact our lives in the world today?

Note to Leader

You can discuss the three areas of the believer's temptation using the chart below.

Temptation—"ism"	Sensualism (self-gratification)	Materialism (self-accumulation)	Egoism (self-glorification)
1 John 2:15–17	Lust of flesh (NIV "cravings")	Lust of eyes	Boastful pride of life
Gen 3:6	"good for food"	"delight to the eyes"	"make one wise"
Matt 4:1–11	"stones to bread"	"have kingdom of world"	"if Son of God"
Entices the desire to . . .	Enjoy	Own	Excel (glory of God or glory of self?)
Expressed in terms of the Christian's enemy	Flesh	World	Devil
Focus on . . .	Doing	Having	Being
Japanese quote—three major problems:	Girls/physical feelings	Gold/fortune	Glitter/fame
Modern-day examples of temptation			
Scriptural answers to temptation	1 Pet 2:11–12 Phil 4:8 1 Thess 4:3 Eph 5:3–13 1 Cor 6:18–20	Phil 4:11–13, 19 1 Tim 6:6–11 1 John 3:17–18	Rom 12:16 Phil 2:3–4 1 Pet 5:6
God's answers to temptation	Purity brings peace	Contentment prevents covetousness	Humility/love forgets self

Chart of Temptation (1 John 2:15–17)

Lesson Six

First John 2:18–27

Discussion Questions

Hook

When you consider or are confronted with cults and false teachers, what is most probably the main point of disagreement that Christian teaching has with the doctrines of such groups?—i.e., how would you most easily discover if they are false teachings—what doctrine(s) would you probe?

Possible Answers

- *Person/work of Christ—his deity and the purpose of his death*
- *What is their authority, especially, what replaces the word of God for them?*
- *Character of God—define God, e.g., the Trinity*
- *The need and ability of man—his sin and inability to satisfy God with good works*
- *Hell and judgment—what do they mean?*
- **Verse** 18: "Children, it is the last hour, and as you have heard that antichrist is coming, so now many antichrists have come. Therefore, we know that it is the last hour."
    - "the last hour"—What does this mean?
        - *The last, desperate stand of Christ's enemies before the final, full redemption*
        - *The time from Christ's resurrection until his return, no matter how long that might take*

- What is meant by the word *antichrist*? Define.
    1. *A substitute, counterfeit Christ, a lying pretender*
    2. *An opponent of Christ (cf. Matt 24:23ff)*
    3. *The gnostics (false teachers of their day)*
- What are the antichrists that we face today?
    - *Humanism, secularism, relativism, evolution, religious cults, worldliness, unbelieving university professors, growing atheism, seemingly anyone who teaches ungodly and unbiblical philosophies, etc.*

Group Exercise

What are the characteristics of the antichrists? Search verses 19–27 for these characteristics:

- **Verse 19:** "They went out from us, but they were not of us; for if they had been of us, they would have continued with us. But they went out, that it might become plain that they all are not of us."
    - *They appear to be believers in the church but are not.*
    - *Antichrists abandon true Christianity.*

Personal Application

Is this verse talking about people losing their salvation?

- **Verses 20–21:** "But you have been anointed by the Holy One, and you all have knowledge. ²¹ I write to you, not because you do not know the truth, but because you know it, and because no lie is of the truth."
    - How can we be sure we are right and following the Lord when others break away from or leave our church or fellowship?
        - *We have the Holy Spirit—v. 20.*
        - *We have God's word, which is true knowledge—v. 21.*
            - *We already have the truth.*
            - *The false teachers do not have truth; they lie.*
        - *These false teachers (gnostics) said they had special (esoteric or hidden) truth.*

- - ◆ *Know the truth—memorize, study, and meditate upon Scripture.*
  - ◆ *I once knew a twenty-year-old who told me that she was able to recognize falsehood by comparing it's teachings to the teaching in the Apostles' Creed.*
  - ▪ What is meant by anointing?
    The Holy Spirit's presence and work in their lives
- **Verse 22:** "Who is the liar but he who denies that Jesus is the Christ? This is the antichrist, he who denies the Father and the Son."
  - ▪ What makes lying so serious?
  - ▪ What are some of the common lies in our culture?
  - ▪ What do you think is the most serious lie possible?
    Denying Christ's deity
  - ▪ Why are they denying the Father and the Son when they deny Jesus is the Christ (cf. John 5:22–23)?
  - ▪ Why is lying evil?

  Possible Answers

  - ◆ *It creates distrust.*
  - ◆ *It brings negative consequences and hurts others.*
  - ◆ *It damages relationships.*
  - ◆ *It is against the truth.*
- **Verse 23:** "No one who denies the Son has the Father. Whoever confesses the Son has the Father also."
  - ▪ In what ways do Christians deny the Son?
    - ◆ *We don't confess him before others.*
    - ◆ *We know something is wrong or sinful and we willfully do it anyhow, shaming the name Christian.*
    - ◆ *We do hypocritical things.*
    - ◆ *We fail to worship and fellowship with other believers, thus denying Christ's call to unity.*
  - ▪ Can a person deny Christ and still be a believer (cf. 1 Cor 12:3)?

Personal Application

Consider Peter's denial of Christ after Christ's arrest. (cf. Mark 14:66–72).

Note to Leader

Address apostasy vs. shame and failure.

- What do you think John means by the word *deny* in this text?
  - *To say that God and man were not united in one person—Christ, who is divine*
  - *To say that Christ did not appear in the flesh*
  - *To say that Christ did not actually die on the cross*

Personal Application

If we fear to mention Christ to others, are we denying him? Why or why not?

- **Verse 24:** "Let what you heard from the beginning abide in you. If what you heard from the beginning abides in you, then you too will abide in the Son and in the Father."
  - How does a person remain safe against heresy?
    - *Staying in the truth*
    - *Listening to sound teachers*
    - *Discerning what he or she hears from others who speak or teach*
  - Why does John keep paralleling Son and Father?
    - *To emphasize the deity of Christ*

Personal Application

- What type of personal devotions are you having?
- Why should they include the word of God?

- **Verse 25:** "And this is the promise that he made to us—eternal life."
  - Define eternal life.
    - When does eternal life begin?
    - What do you think eternal means?

- What does life mean?
        - What will eternal life be like?
    - See John 17:3—how does Jesus define eternal life?

    PERSONAL APPLICATION
    - What does it mean to know Christ?
    - How do we grow in intimacy with (i.e., knowing) Christ?
- **Verse 26:** "I write these things to you about those who are trying to deceive you."
    - How do false teachers lead astray? Discuss methods of deceivers.
    - Why do false teachers try to lead believers astray? Discuss motives of deceivers.
- **Verse 27:** "But the anointing that you received from him abides in you, and you have no need that anyone should teach you. But as his anointing teaches you about everything, and is true, and is no lie—just as it has taught you, abide in him."
    - What is the anointing? *The Holy Spirit*
    - What does he mean, "You have no need that anyone should teach you?" (Consider that the apostle John is presently teaching them in this letter. Also see the following passages: Acts 2:42; 5:42; 2 Tim 2:24; Eph 4:11.)

    POSSIBLE ANSWERS
    - *He is speaking about these false teachers.*
    - *He is telling them not to rely on men alone to teach them.*
    - *Discover what you believe for yourself by studying Scripture.*

    PERSONAL APPLICATION
    What keeps us from studying the Scriptures for ourselves?

Lesson Seven

First John 2:28—3:10

Discussion Questions

Hook

When we consider (or mention) the second coming, or the return, of Christ, what are the responses we might have to the possibility of his soon return?

Possible Answers

Expectation, excitement, fear, purity in life, preparation, worry, concern for others

- How do these responses differ for believers and unbelievers?

Optional Questions

Why do Christians so infrequently study or discuss Christ's second coming? Why do Christians seem at times to be obsessed with Christ's second coming?

First John 2:28—3:3: Christ's Return—Our Response

Chapter 2

- **Verse 28:** "And now, little children, abide in him, so that when he appears we may have confidence and not shrink from him in shame at his coming."
    - **Context:** Living in the face of the antichrist deception

Appendix One

- What does it mean to abide in him?
  - *To continually fellowship with him and to live by his word (cf. John 15:1–5—consider the relationship of the vine to the branch)*

  PERSONAL APPLICATION

  How do we abide in Christ?
  - *Quiet time; must be in the word of God; fellowship with his church and other believers; worship; relying upon the Holy Spirit continuously*
- How does abiding in him give us confidence at his coming? What type of confidence is this?
  - *We should have fewer questions about our assurance of salvation; we have been walking by faith with him already; we are reassured of his presence in our daily walks; we haven't been living in outright or questionable sin.*
- Might believers be ashamed at his coming? What attitudes or practices can cause a believer shame at his coming?
  - *Disobedience; sluggish Christian living; silence in one's Christian testimony; hidden sins; ignoring worship and Christian fellowship in Christ's church*
- Do you agree with this quote by missionary C. T. Studd: "Only one life, 'twill soon be past / Only what's done for Christ will last"?[1]

- **Verse 29:** "If you know that he is righteous, you may be sure that everyone who practices righteousness has been born of him."
  - Who is the he?
  - What does it mean to be righteous?
    - Answers:
      1. *Perfect conformity to God's character*
      2. *Perfect obedience to God*
      3. *Perfect acceptance before God*

---

1. Studd, "Only One Life."

- Is there a difference between being perfectly righteous (like Christ) and being righteous in a more human sense? What would you say is the difference?
  - Answers
    1. *Seeking conformity to God's character*
    2. *Seeking to obey God in all of life*
    3. *Seeking to live in a manner worthy of the name of Christ*
- *John's logic:* The Father is righteous. ∴ Those born of him live righteously, i.e., bear his character and seek to continue in Christlikeness.
- Why are Christians uncomfortable calling themselves righteous? Are we righteous or unrighteous?

Chapter 3

- **Verse 1:** "See what kind of love the Father has given to us, that we should be called children of God; and so we are. The reason why the world does not know us is that it did not know him."
  - Why is it that God's love is magnified (i.e., using the phrase "what kind," meaning it is special) in making us children of God?
    - *God's amazing adoption of us as sinners (cf. Rom 5:6–10: ungodly, sinners, enemies)*
  - Does God love believers more than unbelievers? If so, in what ways?
    - *God has a general love for all people, but a special love for those whom he has saved. He is a father to those whom he has adopted.*
  - As children of God, what types of relationships should we have with our brothers and sisters?
  - How about with other members of the church who are different from us or whom we just don't like/enjoy?
  - How ought a child relate to his or her parents? How is this similar to or different from relating as a child of God as our heavenly Father?

- Discuss the phrase "the world does not know us." How does the world not know us?
  - *They don't value or understand the cross.*
  - *They don't understand spiritual things; these matters are hidden from them.*
  - *They don't receive us as God's work, just as they rejected (did not know) Christ.*
- How do unbelievers try to explain Christianity and conversions to Christ? How do they try to explain Christ?
  - *Psychological in nature*
  - *Emotional*
  - *Manipulated by others*
  - *Reaction to guilt feelings*
  - *Weak and hurting with great needs*
  - *Need a crutch to get them through life*

Read verses 2–3 (purify yourselves).

- **Verse 2:** "Beloved, we are God's children now, and what we will be has not yet appeared; but we know that when he appears we shall be like him, because we shall see him as he is."
  - What is our hope for future glory?
    - *We shall be like him.*
  - In what ways will we be like Christ?
    - *Not as God: eternal, infinite, omnipresent, omnipotent (these are known as God's incommunicable attributes, characteristics of God that man cannot understand or become)*
    - *But as God: pure, holy, righteous, loving, good (communicable attributes)*
- **Verse 3:** "And everyone who thus hopes in him purifies himself as he is pure."
  - What is Christian purity or holiness?

PERSONAL APPLICATION

How do we make ourselves pure?

- What makes you impure (or with what impurities do we naturally battle)?
- (Remember that the gnostics justified sinning in the body as long as the spirit was okay.)

First John 3:4–7: Purity = Not Sinning; Sin's Nature = Lawlessness

- **Verse 4:** "Everyone who makes a practice of sinning also practices lawlessness; sin is lawlessness."
  - What do we normally think of as the worst sins possible to commit?
  - Is all sin equal in God's sight, or are some sins worse than others?
    - *Yes, all sin = lawlessness*
    - *Yet some sins are more serious/heinous than others (murder is worse than thinking about murder or even simply hating another person).*

  PERSONAL APPLICATION

  What is the lawlessness we see each day in our world or our lives? What is the lawlessness we commit each day?
  - What does it mean to practice sin?
    - *Some say that practicing sin means to plan, enjoy, and continue to sin, i.e., sinning regularly or casually without repentance, conviction, or guilt before the Lord.*
- **Verse 5:** "You know that he appeared in order to take away sins, and in him there is no sin."
  - What are the reasons given in verse 5 as to why sin is contrary to Christ? What do they tell us about Christ?
    - *His purpose/work—Christ came to take away sin (cf. 1 Pet 2:24).*

- - *His nature—Christ has no sin.*
  - What does take away sin mean?
    - *To cleanse us from our unrighteousness*
    - *To remove our guilt*
    - *To forgive us of our sins*
    - *To nail our sins to the cross of Christ—they're gone*
  - What would it mean if Christ had sinned?
    - *He would not be God.*
    - *His sacrifice for sins would be imperfect and useless.*

  PERSONAL APPLICATION

  What are the most ungodly influences in our lives today?

- **Verse 6:** "No one who abides in him keeps on sinning; no one who keeps on sinning has either seen him or known him."
  - What does "keeps on sinning" mean?
    Remember the answers above. To practice sin =
    - *Plan—desire to be the god of our lives or of the moment*
    - *Enjoy—no conviction by the Holy Spirit; sin is an ongoing pleasure*
    - *Continue—no repentance of the sinful habit or practices*
- **Verse 7:** "Little children, let no one deceive you. Whoever practices righteousness is righteous, as he is righteous."
  - ***Review:***
    - Who was trying to lead these believers astray?
      - *False gnostic teachers*
    - What problem was John addressing in these churches?
      The problem—the gnostics felt that sinning in/with the body was okay, as long as the spirit wasn't involved; therefore, immoral behavior is okay, if you think it doesn't bother your spirit/soul, etc.
  - What best motivates us to live righteously?
    - *Love of God*

- Confidence that godliness brings spiritual blessing
- Doing right brings a guilt-free conscience
- What are examples of unrighteous living?

  POSSIBLE ANSWERS
  - Sexual immorality—pre-marital sex/pornography/adultery, etc.
  - Cheating/lying/deception
  - Foul language/slander/gossip/using God's name in an empty manner
  - Violating the Ten Commandments in spirit and act
  - Others . . .

First John 3: 8–10: Sin's Origin: Satan

- **Verse 8:** "Whoever makes a practice of sinning is of the devil, for the devil has been sinning from the beginning. The reason the Son of God appeared was to destroy the works of the devil."
  - What was the devil's sin?
    - *Pride/rebellion (see Ezek 28:11–19—the ruler of Tyre is a picture of Satan; Isa 14:12–15—the king of Babylon is a picture of Satan).*
  - From where did sin come?
    - *Answer:*
      1. *Satan: pride in his glory and rebellion in his spirit*
      2. *Man: although created in holiness, innocence, and righteousness, in God's inscrutable plan, man was able/free to sin and fell into sin due to the tempter's efforts.*
  - Logic: practice of sin = character of the devil (cf. John 8:44)
  - What are the works of the devil?
    - *Rebellion against God—in one word, evil*
    - *To defy and replace God in human's lives*
    - *To lie, deceive (blind), and destroy*

Appendix One

- *To hate and create hatred*

Personal Application

How does the devil work in our lives and the lives of those around us? What are examples of his destructive ways?

- Why do modern people not believe in the devil? What are some of the false caricatures of the devil?
- Why do Christians believe in the devil?

- **Verse 9:** "No one born of God makes a practice of sinning, for God's seed abides in him, and he cannot keep on sinning because he has been born of God."
  - What is the seed?

Possible Answers

God's nature (other ideas: the word of God, the Spirit)

- What does it mean that they cannot go on sinning?
  (See answers above for 1 John 3:4, 6.)
  Also, the believer has a new nature that is done with sin. The believer is no longer under bondage to sin. The believer has a new nature and a new will/ability that pursues righteousness (cf. 2 Cor 5:17).

- **Verse 10:** "By this it is evident who are the children of God, and who are the children of the devil: whoever does not practice righteousness is not of God, nor is the one who does not love his brother."
  - The obvious distinction: what are the two tests/proofs of a true believer in this verse?
    - *Moral test—do what is right.*
    - *Social test—love your brother and sister.*
  - Note the black-and-white distinctions: believer or unbeliever—no middle group! How do we respond to that thought?

Lesson Eight

First John 3:11–18

Discussion Questions

Hook

Consider the word *love*. How does western culture (from TV, movies, magazines, music, media, videos, etc.) define or measure love?—i.e., what is love for the unbeliever? How does one know if he or she loves, or is in love?

- **Verse 11:** "For this is the message that you have heard from the beginning, that we should love one another."
  - Here the principle of love is positively stated: "Love one another . . ."

  PERSONAL APPLICATION

  What keeps us from loving one another?

- **Verse 12:** "We should not be like Cain, who was of the evil one and murdered his brother. And why did he murder him? Because his own deeds were evil and his brother's righteous."
  - Here is the principle negatively stated: "Don't be like Cain . . ."
  - What does the text tell us about Cain?
    - *He was of the evil one.*
      - Can an evil person love? Explain an evil person's love. *Yes, but not in the full sense of agape love. Self-investment or self-benefit may be the underlying motive.*
    - *He slew his brother.*
    - *His deeds (actions) were evil.*

Appendix One

- Read Gen 4:2–8 for the story of Cain and Abel.
  - How is Cain characterized in these verses?
  - Why did God accept Abel's offering and not Cain's?

    ### Possible Answers
    - *Cain's heart is wrong ("of the evil one"); the text says, "but for Cain and his offering he [God] had no regard" (4:5).*
    - *Abel offers in faith (see Heb 11:4).*
    - *Abel offers the best.*

    ### Personal Application
    - What sorts of activities or aspects of ministry do Christians get involved in?
      - *Bible study, prayer, church, worship, fellowship, service, mercy*
    - What types of attitudes (negative or positive) do we often display when involved in these type of activities?
    - Why is it that Christians often do these with the wrong attitude(s)?
    - What needs to be changed in order to have a better, God-honoring attitude?
- What is the progression of Cain's murder?
  - *Hypocritical offering*
  - *Anger*
  - *Despondency/digression*
  - *Murder—the first murder*
- Why did Cain kill (slaughter) Abel?
  Because he was jealous of Abel's righteous deeds
- What do you think he was saying to himself when he saw Abel's acceptance?

- **Verse 13:** "Do not be surprised, brothers, that the world hates you."

- John is saying that if we live righteously we should not be surprised if the world hates us.
- Are you hated (or rejected/persecuted) by anyone in the world? Why do you think Christians are hated in the western world?
- Conversely, why are Christians not hated in America or in our cultural context?
  - *Government still retains some respect for God and/or religion (although this appears to be changing).*
  - *The church isn't proclaiming Christ.*
  - *Christ is just a good/nice thing.*
  - *Tolerance*
  - *Other . . .*
- What is it about the Christian message that should cause the world to hate us?
  - *We claim that there is only one way of salvation.*
  - *We speak against evil cultural practices.*
  - *We call for godly living.*
- Do any of you have an illustration of being hated or persecuted by the world in your life for being a Christian (at any time)?
- What qualities about your life, lifestyle, or beliefs (in your job, neighborhood, campus, leisure, etc.) could cause someone to ridicule you as a Christian?

- **Verse 14:** "We know that we have passed out of death into life, because we love the brothers. Whoever does not love abides in death."
  - The word used in the passage for love is *agape*. What is this agape love (cf. 1 Cor 13—also, see v. 16)?
  - What are the attitudes in our hearts that keep us from loving fellow Christians?

    POSSIBLE ANSWERS

    Jealousy; personality differences; doctrinal disagreements; envy; pride; first impressions; others don't associate with them; prejudice and/or racism; political issues; socioeconomic differences, etc.

- Think of one person whom you have the most difficulty loving (don't name them); what is one kind act of love you could do to help him or her? (Do it!)
- **Verse 15:** "Everyone who hates his brother is a murderer, and you know that no murderer has eternal life abiding in him."
  - See Matt 5:21–25—the issue of reconciling love
  - Why do Christians not approach brothers and sisters whom they have hurt or who have hurt them in order to be reconciled?

    POSSIBLE ANSWERS
    - *They don't understand true forgiveness.*
    - *They are afraid.*
    - *They can't be transparent.*
    - *They are living in sin and won't obey.*
    - *They can't trust the other person.*
    - *They have never seen it modeled by someone else.*
  - What are some ways in which we reject our brothers and sisters even if we do not actually hate them?

    POSSIBLE ANSWERS
    - *We avoid them.*
    - *We don't listen or aren't sensitive to their needs.*
    - *We fail to pray for them.*
    - *We put them down, either directly or behind their backs.*
- **Verse 16:** "By this we know love, that he laid down his life for us, and we ought to lay down our lives for the brothers."

  PERSONAL APPLICATION

  How do we lay down our lives for our brothers and sisters?

  POSSIBLE ANSWERS
  - *Pray for them.*

- *Call, text, email, or message them and encourage them in some way.*
- *Be available, despite our busy schedule; give up our time.*
- *Befriend them.*
- *Give them a ride to church, the grocery store, post office, hospital, or similar needs.*
- *Reach out to visitors in our church or group.*
- *Give them counsel—a listening and nonjudgmental ear.*
- *Show up in times of need.*
- *Provide help in their financial struggles.*
- *Visit them when they are in need.*

- **Verse 17:** "But if anyone has the world's goods and sees his brother in need, yet closes his heart against him, how does God's love abide in him?"
  - How does verse 17 relate to verse 16 above?
  Verse 17 is an example of how to lay down your life for others.
  - In what ways is the Christian life or body of Christ communal?
  - Is this type of communal living the norm for today's church? (See Acts 2:44–45 and Acts 4:32–35.)
    - *Answer: these were special circumstances in the life of the early church where out-of-town new believers could not continue to remain in Jerusalem after the Pentecostal falling of the Holy Spirit, unless they were assisted by other believers.*
  - Why do we hold back on pity (close our hearts) for others or choose not to help them out in their time of need?
  - Can a Christian have too much pity on or compassion for others?
  - Can a person have pity on others but still not have the love of God in the heart? How could that happen?
  - The point: If you have/possess what can meet a brother's need and it is expendable (even at sacrifice) and you hold back, then *your* heart has a problem: no love for God.
    - *See Jas 2:14–16.*

- **Verse 18:** "Little children, let us not love in word or talk but in deed and in truth."
  - Do you agree with this statement: "Loving in word and tongue = human love; loving in deed and truth = God's love"?
  - What does loving in truth mean?
    - *According to God's word*
    - *Genuine, not just in thought*
    - *Loving according to your promise to help*
    - *Not hypocritical but in true action*

Lesson Nine

First John 4:1–6

Discussion Questions

Hook

Look at (read) and then study the passage. What words or phrases are repeated?
Spirit/from God/world
What is the passage about?
Or ask these questions: Is judging others always wrong? When should we judge others?

- **Verse 1:** "Beloved, do not believe every spirit, but test the spirits to see whether they are from God, for many false prophets have gone out into the world."
    - Why the admonition to "not believe every spirit"?
        - *The gnostic heretics are trying to wrongly influence these early Christian believers. These readers must discern what they are hearing.*
    - How is this verse related to 2:24 ("Let what you heard from the beginning abide in you. If what you heard from the beginning abides in you, then you too will abide in the Son and in the Father")?
        - *Human teachers can threaten a believer's abiding in Christ.*
    - What does John mean by the spirits?
    The spiritual realities behind the teaching and lives of others
    - "test the spirits"—How do we test the spirits to see if they are true?
    Question the doctrine of the teachers.

- Which doctrines might John be wanting to test?
  Who is Christ? How does the Christian live?
- What are other doctrines into which believers need to inquire?
  Nature of God/salvation/church/man/sin
  Character of the teachers
- What are some characteristics of bad/false teachers?

  Possible Answers
  - *Divisive—always splitting people and gaining a following*
  - *Legalistic—must follow their manmade rules to be accepted*
  - *One man exalted—appear to be building one's own kingdom*
  - *Anti-family—call people away from the relationships they have with their family*
  - *Require super sacrifice—must give all to the church/ministry and give up all for these groups as well*

- How would a believer recognize a true prophet?
  - *His word comes true.*
  - *His word does not contradict Scripture.*
  - *Cf. Jer 28:9.*
  - *Cf. Deut 18:22.*
- What is a false prophet?
  An individual who leads people to believe in, serve, and worship other gods and practices false teaching.
  - *See Deut 13:1–5.*
- Why do people follow false teachers/cults? What is attractive about such groups?

  Possible Answers

  They receive love and/or direction; the leader or members have charisma; the group gives them a cause; the ministry might be exciting;

the ministry is something different; the group or leader provides purpose, structure, and support.

- **Verse 2:** "By this you know the Spirit of God: every spirit that confesses that Jesus Christ has come in the flesh is from God . . ."
    - According to this verse, how do we identify the person who has the Spirit of God?
        - *Confesses that Jesus has come in the flesh (the incarnation)*
    - Why is the fact that Jesus Christ has come in the flesh important to John's readers?
        - *It is not the message of the gnostics.*
        - *In addition to being God, he must be a human/man who can actually suffer and die for sins, as a sacrifice.*
- **Verse 3:** ". . . and every spirit that does not confess Jesus is not from God. This is the spirit of the antichrist, which you heard was coming and now is in the world already."
    - What is the spirit of the antichrist?

    PROBABLE ANSWERS
    - *An opposition (anti) to Christ's true nature*
    - *A substitution of another gospel that does not affirm the necessity of Christ's deity*
    - When did they hear that the spirit of antichrist was coming?

    POSSIBLE ANSWERS
    - *See 1 John 2:18–29—possibly the coming of the spirit of the antichrist was a common first-century teaching.*
    - *Christ predicted it in Matt 24:3–5.*
- **Verse 4:** "Little children, you are from God and have overcome them, for he who is in you is greater than he who is in the world."
    - What does it mean to overcome false teachers?
        - *To discern that their teaching is false and to turn away from it*
        - *To not follow them intellectually or emotionally in their false teaching*

Appendix One

- ◆ *To not be influenced by them into unbelief or compromise of life or one's actions*
  - As believers, how do we overcome deceptive teachings that confront us?—i.e., what can we do to combat them personally in our own lives?

    POSSIBLE ANSWERS
    - ◆ *Master the word of God.*
    - ◆ *Study apologetics.*
    - ◆ *Read edifying books on cults, etc.*
    - ◆ *Trust the Holy Spirit.*
    - ◆ *Avoid private interpretations, and learn from the mature and doctrinally sound.*

- **Verse 5:** "They are from the world; therefore they speak from the world, and the world listens to them."
  - How does our world speak falsely concerning . . .
    - ◆ Humanity?

      POSSIBLE ANSWERS

      The nature of humanity—how were humans created? Are they sinful? The nature of the soul and the image of God—why does humanity exist?
    - ◆ Morality?
      - What is the moral law? How are we held accountable?
      - What is freedom versus responsibility?
      - What is goodness? Is morality relative?
    - ◆ God?
      - Is he both loving and holy/wrathful?
    - ◆ Evil in the world?
      - How do we explain evil in the world? How do we live with injustice, etc.?
    - ◆ Success?

- *How does the world define success?*
- *How does God define success?*
  - Guilt?
    - *How does humanity overcome its guilt and shame? Is guilt real?*
- **Verse 6:** "We are from God. Whoever knows God listens to us; whoever is not from God does not listen to us. By this we know the Spirit of truth and the spirit of error."
  - What is the apostle John trying to emphasize in verse 6? *He speaks for God. He has authority; therefore, they should listen.*
  - How can he claim such strong authority?
    - *See John 20:19–23: Jesus gives his disciples the power to forgive sins.*
    - *John 14:23–26: Jesus promises his disciples that the Holy Spirit will guide them into all truth.*

Personal Application

- What Bible passages would you take someone to if they asked you to give them an explanation of . . .
  - Christ's deity?
  - The Trinity?
  - The inspiration and authority of Scripture?
- How can we better study and apply the Bible?
  - *Understand the themes of the Bible and the individual books.*
  - *Learn to use a concordance (or cross-references) and a Bible dictionary.*
  - *Read a book covering a biblical survey or overview.*
  - *Use biblical commentaries.*
  - *Use daily devotional helps or readings.*

Lesson Ten

First John 4:7–12

Discussion Questions

Hook

Use this exercise to begin. Read verses 7–21 and underline or circle the word *love*. Look for and briefly discuss (if there is time):

1. The character of love
2. Love and its relationship to believers
3. Descriptions of God's love

- **Verse 7:** "Beloved, let us love one another, for love is from God, and whoever loves has been born of God and knows God."
    - "love is from God"—John is saying that love's source is God.
    - Can a non-Christian display true love if love is from God? How? *Humans are made in the image of God. They still retain some of that image.*
    - There are three types of love described in the Greek New Testament:
        - *Eros*—possessive/selfish
        - *Philia*—brotherly
        - *Agape*—unconditional/sacrificial
    - How does knowing God impact the character and quality of our love?
- **Verse 8:** "Anyone who does not love does not know God, because God is love."

- What prevents Christians from loving others with God's love (i.e., fellow employees, classmates, roommates, neighbors, family members, strangers, etc.)?
- Is God love alone?
  - What are other characteristics (attributes) of God?
    Holy, merciful, just, patient, good, powerful, omniscient, omnipresent, omnipotent, infinite, eternal, unchangeable, etc.
  - How do these attributes relate to his love, if in any way?
- Do you think that love is the most important attribute of God? Why or why not?
- What is the danger of God being love only?
- I once heard a minister say, "If God is love, then we can also say 'Love is God.'" How would you respond to that statement?

- **Verse 9:** "In this the love of God was made manifest among us, that God sent his only Son into the world, so that we might live through him."
  - How does John characterize God's love in this verse?
    - *God sent his Son that we might live.*
  - Why do people scoff at this thought, i.e., God sending his Son?
    - Cf. Phil 2:6–8.
  - What was Christ's life like in heaven before the incarnation?
  - In what ways did Christ suffer on earth, thus proving God's great love for us?

  POSSIBLE ANSWERS
  - *He associated with sinners.*
  - *His enemies hated him.*
  - *He was rejected by his people.*
  - *He went through temptation.*
  - *He was humiliated (born lowly).*
  - *He went through loneliness and was forsaken and denied by his own disciples.*

- *His love for men was great, but it was rejected constantly.*
- *Satan hated him and attacked him.*
- *The Pharisees disclaimed him.*
- *His death—God gave his best!*

- What does it mean to live through him? What kind of life does Christ provide for us personally?

POSSIBLE ANSWERS
- *Christ gives us his Spirit.*
- *Christ gives us new, spiritual desires.*
- *Christ gives us the fruit of the Spirit.*
- *Christ gives us hope.*

PERSONAL APPLICATION

How do we grow in the life that Christ promises to give us?
Seek him through his word; walk with him devotionally; rely upon his Holy Spirit; walk by faith; respond to his grace; worship and serve with other believers in his church.

- **Verse 10:** "In this is love, not that we have loved God but that he loved us and sent his Son to be the propitiation for our sins."
  - What is the amazing character of God's love mentioned in this verse?
    - *God loved us, not because we loved him first.*
    - *God's love takes the initiative.*
    - *God loves sinners.*
  - What is there in us that would make God love us?
    Read these passages (as time allows):
    - *1 Cor 1:20, 26–29*
    - *Deut 7:6–7*
    - *Rom 5:6–8*

- How do you develop love for your enemies, or for those who do wrong against you?—i.e., in what ways can you demonstrate love to people who are difficult to love?

    Possible Answers

    - *Pray for them.*
    - *Go out of your way and talk with them.*
    - *Send them a letter, card, email, text, etc., and sincerely compliment them for something you appreciate about them.*
    - *Make, buy, or send a gift for/to them.*
    - *Try to better understand their personality and/or their background.*

- What is an atoning sacrifice?
  God's justice and wrath upon sin satisfied in Christ's death

    - *Illustration:* Our sin traded for Christ's righteousness and our guilt and punishment placed on Christ at the cross (cf. 2 Cor 5:21).
    - *Explanation:* Faith (in Christ's finished work) + nothing = right before God

- **Verse 11:** "Beloved, if God so loved us, we also ought to love one another."

    - What is the conclusion derived from verses 9–11?
      Christ's sacrifice for our justification (atonement/peace with God) should result in love for others (sanctification: our reflection of Christlikeness and spiritual growth).
    - What should we conclude if a person professes belief in the cross and Christ but then is unloving toward others?
    - Quote (anonymous): "No one who has gone to the cross and *experienced* God's love can go back to a life of selfishness."

- **Verse 12:** "No one has ever seen God; if we love one another, God abides in us and his love is perfected in us."

    - Why has no one ever seen God?
        - *God is holy (perfect unapproachability) and a spirit (unseen).*

Appendix One

- *Man has a sin nature.*
- Then how can sinful people know that God exists and loves them?

  ### Possible Answers
  - *They trust in God's grace.*
  - *They always view the cross.*
  - *They see God's kindness toward and patience with them.*
  - *They see God's goodness in his creation.*
  - *They understand that God is willing to reveal himself to them in creation and his word and through his Son.*
- How do non-Christians see God's love in us?
  - *Love = proof of God indwelling the believer*
  - *We love them unconditionally.*
  - *We are gracious to them and treat them well.*
  - *We demonstrate kindness toward them if they offend us.*
- What is perfect love?
  - *Active love = perfected love—love that is made complete*
  - *Active love, especially between believers, is an apologetic for the gospel (John 13:34–35).*

Lesson Eleven

First John 4:13–21

Discussion Questions

Hook

A world-renowned evangelistic presentation (*Everyday Evangelism*, once known as *Evangelism Explosion*) begins by asking this question: "Have you come to a place in your spiritual life where you can say for certain that if you were to die today you would go to heaven?"[2] Surprisingly, many Christians who have been surveyed cannot answer yes to this question. What do you think are some reasons why Christians lack an assurance of their salvation?

Possible Answers

Failure; disobedience (sin in their life); lack of knowing the promises in God's word; false fear of God; little faith in God; immature spiritual growth; don't understand the doctrines of justification, grace, and adoption; don't fully understand the work of Christ; are taught that one cannot ever have assurance or that one can lose her or his salvation

Read 1 John 4:13–21 and look for what God has provided to give believers assurance of salvation (i.e., abiding in him).

- *v. 13 his Spirit*
- *v. 15 our confession of Christ*
- *v. 16 our love (agape)*
- *v. 18 our lack of fear*

2. Kennedy, *Evangelism Explosion*, 31.

Appendix One

Now, let's go back and study each verse . . .

- **Verse 13:** "By this we know that we abide in him and he in us, because he has given us of his Spirit."
  - In what ways does the Holy Spirit witness to us that we belong to God?

  POSSIBLE ANSWERS
  - *Convicts us of sin—John 16:8*
  - *Helps us to pray—Rom 8:26–27*
  - *Gives us a spirit of adoption, crying "Abba/Father"—Rom 8:15*
  - *Reveals the Word to us—John 16:13*
  - *Helps us to believe what the word of God teaches and promises—John 14:26*

  PERSONAL APPLICATION

  Can any of you explain a time when you were studying the word of God and seemed to receive an accurate, clear insight into it (realizing that it was the Holy Spirit's work)?

- **Verses 14–15:** "And we have seen and testify that the Father has sent his Son to be the Savior of the world. ¹⁵ Whoever confesses that Jesus is the Son of God, God abides in him, and he in God."
  - Why is it important that we confess that Jesus is the Son of God? *Jesus is equal with God; he is God himself.*

  NOTE TO LEADER

  The late Dr. David Nicholas, who pastored Spanish River Presbyterian Church in Boca Raton, Florida, for many years, once said that he would often ask people this question: "Would you say that Jesus is the Son of God?" Often they would answer yes. But when he asked them, "Would you say that Jesus is God the Son?," they would frequently say no.[3] What do you think is the difference, if any?

  - Why must Jesus be equal to God?

---

3. Nicholas, *Whatever Happened to the Gospel*, 64–65.

- ◆ *His life must be perfect, so that his sacrifice for sin is perfect. God will not accept an imperfect sacrifice for sin.*
- ◆ *If Christ is not deity (God), then he cannot pay for the sins of the world. Only God could pay for the huge number of sins of billions of people.*

- Has Jesus ever ceased to be equal to God?
  No. However, one might wonder about this question:
  - ◆ What about his not knowing the time of his second (return) coming?
    In his humanity, he limited himself to space (with a body) and time and also limited his knowledge (again, as a man), while always having been fully God (infinite and eternal in nature).

- How do others explain away Christ's deity?
  He was a good man, maybe the greatest man of all time; he was a great teacher; he was crazy; he was a liar; he tried to fulfill prophecy by his own doing; he didn't really do the miracles; he was a phantom; he was a glorious angel with much power (this is the Jehovah's Witnesses view; they completely deny the deity of Christ).

- How do we refute these arguments?
  - ◆ *C. S. Lewis's answer is called the trilemma: Jesus was either crazy or lying or telling the truth (it doesn't answer every question, but is helpful):*
    - *He can't be a lunatic—his life was too godly, impeccable, a great example.*
    - *He can't be a liar—he would have been a hypocrite and a sinner; he told others to be honest, but would he then have died for a lie?*
    - *Since he can't be a lunatic, nor a liar, he must therefore be Lord!*

- **Verses 16–18:** "So we have come to know and to believe the love that God has for us. God is love, and whoever abides in love abides in God, and God abides in him. ¹⁷ By this is love perfected with us, so that we may have confidence for the day of judgment, because as he is so also are we in this world. ¹⁸ There is no fear in love, but perfect love casts out fear. For fear has to do with punishment, and whoever fears has not been perfected in love."

Appendix One

- What does it mean to live in love? How do believers live in love? *Agape love means that the other person is more important than you are. You are willing to sacrifice yourself for the other. You put others before yourself and are committed to loving (and forgiving) and serving them, no matter what they do to you.*

- Why do people fear God? Should they fear God?
  - *His judgment = true fear.*
  - *They think he will hurt them = false fear.*
  - *They do not understand that his discipline (for sin) in their lives is for their good and because of his love (Heb 12:7–11).*

- In what ways, if any, should Christians fear God? Put another way, should they never fear him?

Possible Answers

  - *We must fear him in reverence of his holiness.*
  - *We must fear him if we are living in blatant sin.*
  - *We should fear him, because he might discipline us for our sin if we don't repent.*
  - *We should not fear him in thinking that he will judge/punish us for our guilt; Christ took our punishment on the cross.*
  - *We should not fear him in thinking that he will harm us.*
  - *Cf. Rom 8:28; Jer 29:11.*

- How does God's love get rid of our fears?
  - *Gal 4:6—We call him Father (Abba is a term of affection).*
  - *Heb 12:6–7—God's discipline is motivated by his love for us.*

- **Verse 19:** "We love because he first loved us."
  - How has God loved us first? What are the various ways God shows his love for us?
    - Point: agape love is in us, because God first "agaped" us. His love for us precedes our love for him.

- **Verses 20–21:** "If anyone says, 'I love God,' and hates his brother, he is a liar; for he who does not love his brother whom he has seen cannot love God whom he has not seen. ²¹ And this commandment we have from him: whoever loves God must also love his brother."

- What are some examples of hatred in our society?
- How do people justify their hatred for another?

   POSSIBLE ANSWERS:
   - *Their actions deserve hatred.*
   - *I have righteous indignation toward them.*
   - *They badly hurt someone I love deeply.*
   - *They are obnoxious and unlikable.*

- What is the difference between dislike and hate? How do we keep from hating the person(s) we dislike? How do we love the person we dislike?
- Note the apostle John's teaching on being a liar and not a believer (involving the three themes of the book, as related to assurance):
   - 4:20: *Love*—you say you love God, but you do not love your brother = liar
   - 1:6; 2:4: *Righteousness*—you say you have fellowship with God, but you walk in darkness (practice sin) = liar
   - 2:22,23: *Truth*—you say you possess God, but you deny Christ's deity = liar

Lesson Twelve

First John 5:1–5

Discussion Questions

Hook

What makes you (or any believer) want to quit in the Christian life? When you are discouraged about your day-to-day life and your personal walk with God and/or when you wonder (or doubt) whether the sacrifice of being a Christian is worth it all, what keeps you going (i.e., what motivates you)? *The bottom line is faith (1 John 5:4–5), and we will look at the topic of faith in this passage.*

- Read verses 1–5. Look for the three themes:
    - Truth/belief (vv. 1, 4–5)
    - Love (vv. 1–2)
    - Righteousness/commands (vv. 2–3)

Overview:

- What does John say about
    - Truth (belief or faith in God's truth)
        - *v. 1: Belief = proof of adoption*
        - *v. 4: Faith—overcomes the world*
        - *v. 5: Faith in Christ—overcomes the world*
    - Love
        - *v. 1: If you love the Father, you love his children.*

- *v. 2: Love of God proves (and provides) love of his children.*
- *v. 3: Love of God = obedience*
- Righteousness
  - *v. 2: Love of God's children must be according to the word of God*
  - *v. 3: Love of God's children = obedience/joy to obey*

Discussion

- **Verse 1:** "Everyone who believes that Jesus is the Christ has been born of God, and everyone who loves the Father loves whoever has been born of him."
  - Discuss relationships of brothers/sisters (siblings) growing up together—bad and good.
  - What are the differences that usually prevent Christians from loving one another, even though they are members of the same spiritual family?

    POSSIBLE ANSWERS
    - *Doctrinal—don't believe the same things, especially in gray areas and nonessential doctrines*
    - *Relational—don't like being around the other person; they're too different, both in personalities and interests*
    - *Functional/practical—can't work together*
  - Why do these differences split Christians? When are these differences good? When do they become bad?
    - *Good, if you can agree to disagree and want to remain united in Christ while still loving one another*
    - *Bad, if believers cannot love one another, are divisive, or try to destroy one another*
  - Is there any Christian (no names or hints, please) whom you know you cannot love? Why?

Appendix One

- How do we love by faith? What is there that we believe about God and scriptural truths that enables us to love others by faith and not by how we might feel about them?

  ###### Possible Answers

  - *God loved us, even when we were his enemies.*
  - *God gives us the fruit of the Spirit, especially love, patience, kindness, gentleness, and goodness.*
  - *God calls us to endlessly forgive those who wrong us.*
  - *God is sovereign, and he has placed this person(s) in my life for a reason.*
  - *God calls us to pray for everyone and particularly for our enemies.*
  - *God calls us to humble ourselves and serve others.*

  ###### Personal Application

  What are some practical ways to love those whom you struggle to love?

  ###### Possible Answers

  - *Make a list of those you have difficulty loving (keep it short).*
  - *Pray for them.*
  - *Give a gift to or do something special for them.*
  - *Tell them you love them—surprise them!*

- **Verse 2:** "By this we know that we love the children of God, when we love God and obey his commandments."
  - Our love for God's children is based on what two things?
    - *Agape/God's love—love for God and his love for us*
    - *Carrying out God's commands*
  - How does carrying out God's commands help us know that we love the children of God?

Possible Answers

- ◆ God's word/commands

  - *John 15:13:* "Greater love has no one than this, that someone lay down his life for his friends."

  - *Matt 5:43–44:* "You have heard that it was said, 'You shall love your neighbor and hate your enemy.' ⁴⁴But I say to you, 'Love your enemies and pray for those who persecute you . . . '"

  - *Gal 5:13–15:* "For you were called to freedom, brothers. Only do not use your freedom as an opportunity for the flesh, but through love serve one another. ¹⁴For the whole law is fulfilled in one word: 'You shall love your neighbor as yourself.' ¹⁵ But if you bite and devour one another, watch out that you are not consumed by one another."

  - *Gal 6:1–2:* "Brothers, if anyone is caught in any transgression, you who are spiritual should restore him in a spirit of gentleness. Keep watch on yourself, lest you too be tempted. ²Bear one another's burdens, and so fulfill the law of Christ."

  Personal Application

  Why don't we rebuke, exhort, and comfort one another? How is the ministry of rebuke an act of love? How should we do these things: rebuke, exhort, and comfort?

  - *Eph 4:31–32:* "Let all bitterness and wrath and anger and clamor and slander be put away from you, along with all malice. ³²Be kind to one another, tenderhearted, forgiving one another, as God in Christ forgave you."

- ▪ What is false love? How is it expressed?
  Insincere, manipulative, temporal, uncommitted, self-invested

- **Verse 3:** "For this is the love of God, that we keep his commandments. And his commandments are not burdensome."

  - ▪ Why would John say, "God's commands are not burdensome? Don't most people seem to think that God's commands are an intrusion into their lives?

Appendix One

- Consider the Ten Commandments in Exod 20:1–17.
  - Which of these commands do you think non-Christians would dislike the most?
  - Which would non-Christians consider to be the most difficult to keep? Christians?
- Why would non-Christians dislike doing/obeying God's commands?

POSSIBLE ANSWERS

- *They don't see the importance or benefit (or value) in keeping God's commands.*
- *They don't perceive the spiritual joy and peace that come from obedience (cf. Ps 119:16).*
- *They don't think about (meditate on) God's commands much (cf. Ps 119:47–48).*
- *They sense the burden of legalism (cf. Matt 23:1–7—the burden of the laws of the Pharisees).*

- In what ways are following/keeping God's commands freeing for the believer?

- **Verse 4:** "For everyone who has been born of God overcomes the world. And this is the victory that has overcome the world—our faith."
  - What does to overcome the world mean?

POSSIBLE ANSWERS

- *To not fall into sin*
- *To not act like, or believe like, the unbelieving world*
- *To have victory in the Christian life*
- *To walk with Christ until the end of our lives*

  - What does this verse say about a Christian losing salvation?
    - *We are born of God; therefore, we are in his family as a secure family member.*
    - *We are born of God; therefore, we will gain the victory over the temptations and lures of an ungodly world.*

- ◆ *God's true children will overcome the (fallen and evil) world.*
- What does it mean to have faith? How does faith help us to overcome the world that is posed against us?

POSSIBLE ANSWER:

Faith = believing God will prevail and take care of us.

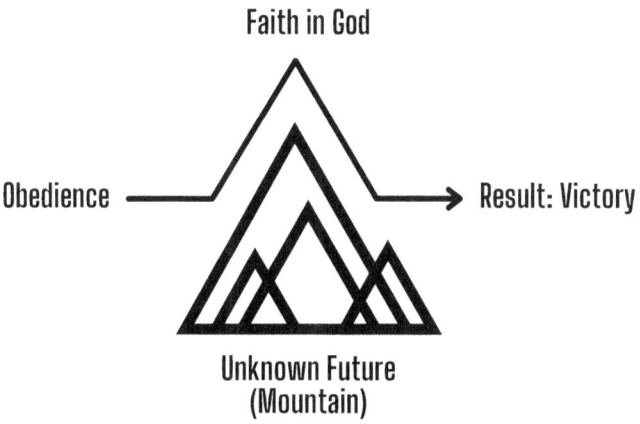

Figure 4: Overcoming Faith (1 John 5:4)

- In what ways (examples/possibilities) have you seen God prevail as you have trusted him? Are there other stories you have seen or heard about God's victories in believers' lives?
- **Verse 5:** "Who is it that overcomes the world except the one who believes that Jesus is the Son of God?"
  - How does believing that Jesus is the Son of God help us overcome (or conquor) the world?
  - Why do unbelievers not overcome the world?
    - ◆ See Rev 2:7, 11, 17, 26–27; 3:5, 12, 21; 21:5–7.

Lesson Thirteen

First John 5:6–12

Discussion Questions

Hook

If you had to stand on trial in a court in order to defend the truth or validity of Christianity, what evidence would you give that Christianity, or Christ, is of God?

Brief Exercise

- Look at verses 6–12: what evidence does God give us concerning Christ? Underline the word *witness*.

    Note to Leader

    This is considered by most commentators to be the most perplexing section of the epistle.

Discussion

- **Verse 6:** "This is he who came by water and blood—Jesus Christ; not by the water only but by the water and the blood. And the Spirit is the one who testifies, because the Spirit is the truth."
    - What comes to mind when you think of water and blood in regard to Christ?

Probable Answers

- *Water could speak of his birth, or it could speak of his baptism.*
- *Blood most certainly speaks of his death on the cross.*
- *Other interpretations:*
  - *Augustine: John 19:34-35—spear: blood and water from side of Jesus*
  - *Calvin/Luther: the two sacraments*
- Why are these (baptism, death) important in Christ's life?
  - Baptism (water)—cf. Matt 3:13-17 (Christ's baptism).
  - *Jesus is being commissioned and empowered for his work.*
    - *Cf. Num 8:6-7—sprinkling/cleansing.*
    - *Cf. Num 4:3,47—initiation into priestly duties.*
    - *Cf. Luke 3:23 (thirty years of age—priestly service?).*
  - Death (blood)—cf. Heb 10:11-15,19.
    - *His finished work for our salvation—atonement for sins*
    - *Justification for believers*
- *Helpful/Insightful Background*
  - The Corinthian gnostics believed the following: Jesus was a mere man, born of Joseph and Mary in natural wedlock. Christ descended upon him at baptism and departed again at the cross.
  - John is trying to combat this false idea.
- **Verses 7-8**: "For there are three that testify: [8] the Spirit and the water and the blood; and these three agree."
  - There are two types of testimony regarding Christ:
    - History—water and blood
    - Experiential—the Spirit
  - How many witnesses are needed to testify that something is true? Cf. the number of witnesses needed (Deut 19:15).

Appendix One

Personal Application

We should not believe one-witness gossip!

- Why is the phrase "and these three are in agreement" important?

Probable Answer

- *The gnostics are not in agreement with the Spirit, since they believe that a spirit being descended upon the human Jesus in a temporary fashion (at his baptism, departing prior to his death on the cross).*

- Why do you think the author changes the order of witnesses in verse 8 (as opposed to verse 6)?

Possible Answers

- *The Spirit is present and active now in their lives—Christ's work is in the past.*
- *The Spirit gives power/assurance to the testimony in their lives.*

- **Verse 9:** "If we receive the testimony of men, the testimony of God is greater, for this is the testimony of God that he has borne concerning his Son."
  - What is the logic and thrust of verse 9?

- **Verse 10:** "Whoever believes in the Son of God has the testimony in himself. Whoever does not believe God has made him a liar, because he has not believed in the testimony that God has borne concerning his Son."
  - What is the function of witnesses, i.e., what do witnesses normally try to cause us to do?
    - *Believe the facts.*
  - How do people sin against God when they don't believe his witness?
    - *They call him a liar.*
    - *They are rebelling against God's entire work.*
  - What characteristics of God are they attacking (e.g., in the issue of whether Scripture is inspired)?

Possible Answers

- *His truthfulness*
- *His faithfulness*
- *His omniscience and omnipotence (ability to easily reveal himself through revelation/Scripture)*
- *His moral purity and perfection*

- **Verses 11–12:** "And this is the testimony, that God gave us eternal life, and this life is in his Son. ¹² Whoever has the Son has life; whoever does not have the Son of God does not have life."

  - What does eternal life look like? How does being a Christian, i.e., being one who has eternal life, make believers attractive to others?
  - What is the whole purpose of God's testimony/witness?
    To give us eternal life
  - How does belonging to Christ give the believer assurance of salvation/eternal life?
  - How does having assurance of eternal life impact our daily lives?
  - What disturbs our assurance?

  Note to Leader

  See the Hook/Introduction to Lesson Eleven above (it never hurts to talk more about the topic of assurance of salvation, especially since verses 11–13 focus on the primary purpose of the book of 1 John).

  - What do we do when attacked by doubts?

  Possible Answers

  - *Obey what we know or believe to be true.*
  - *Read more Scripture, trusting God to encourage you.*
  - *Study the word of God, especially those questions that are causing your doubts; seek God's answers.*
  - *Pray that the Lord will encourage you.*
  - *Find someone who can help by answering your honest questions.*

- What do verses 11–12 tell us about eternal life?
  - *It is given—a gift, not earned.*
  - *It is in His Son—only in Christ, who is God the Son.*
  - *The believer has the life—a present possession.*

Lesson Fourteen

First John 5:13–21

Discussion Questions

Initial Discussion

- The context of this passage is the preceding verses—1 John 5:7–12.
    - What is the main thrust of 5:7–12?
    It speaks of witnesses and testimonies.
    - What do witnesses provide?
    Truth, proof, evidence, corroboration
- Therefore, John is saying, "with these witnesses in mind, be assured of the following . . ."

Hook:

Read verses 13–21. Underline the word *know*.

- What can we know for certain? (Answers below will list some certainties that believers in Christ possess.)

- **Verse 13:** "I write these things to you who believe in the name of the Son of God that you may know that you have eternal life."
    - What are "these things"?
        - *Most probably the entire letter*
    - Why would John be writing to give these believers assurance? Why and what were they questioning?

Appendix One

Possible Answers

- *Is what they believe real or true?*
- *Was/is Jesus truly the Messiah, i.e., the God-man?*
- *Is what they have experienced through hearing the gospel true?*
- *Do they really have eternal life (the gnostic heretics may have been sowing seeds of doubt in their minds)?*

- Certainty 1: The primary purpose of the book is to give these believers a sense of certainty. John wants to let them know that those who believe in Christ have eternal life; this is the basic (main) purpose of the book of 1 John.
  - Other purposes of the book: cf. 1:3–4; 2:1, 12–14, 21, 26.

- **Verses 14–15:** "And this is the confidence that we have toward him, that if we ask anything according to his will he hears us. ¹⁵ And if we know that he hears us in whatever we ask, we know that we have the requests that we have asked of him."
  - What are the certainties that we see expressed in these two verses?
  - Certainty 2: We know that God hears our prayers.
  - Certainty 3: We know that God answers the prayers he hears.
  - Why do non-Christians fail to pray?

Possible Answers

- *They lack a sense of indebtedness.*
- *They have a spirit of ingratitude.*
- *They do not know God (or believe in him).*
- *They have no faith.*
- *They have no divine life.*
- *They are self-dependent.*
- *They have not experienced God's grace in their lives.*

- Why do Christians fail to pray?

Possible Answers

- *They lack a sense of indebtedness.*

- *They are lazy.*
- *They don't understand the importance or need of prayer.*
- *They try to live the Christian life in their own strength.*
- What are the proper elements/parts of prayer?

  POSSIBLE ANSWERS
  - *See the Lord's prayer in Matt 6:7–13.*
  - *Martin Luther, in a work on the Lord's Prayer, developed what became an acrostic for prayer:*
    - *A = Adoration*
    - *C = Confession*
    - *T = Thanksgiving*
    - *S = Supplication*
- How does God answer our prayers?—i.e., what are the various answers we might expect?
  - *Yes, no, wait, some other way.*
- What are some possible examples of prayers that are not aligned with God's expressed will?
- *Note:* Here is a quote from the late Dr. John Stott: "Every true prayer is a variation on the theme 'Thy will be done.'"[4]

  PERSONAL APPLICATION

  We don't try to change God's mind or impose our will on him. We must pray according to his word.

- **Verse 16:** "If anyone sees his brother committing a sin not leading to death, he shall ask, and God will give him life—to those who commit sins that do not lead to death. There is sin that leads to death; I do not say that one should pray for that."
  - *Note:* This is a special intercessory prayer. It is difficult to know or guess what exactly the apostle John is speaking about (context: "Now that you've experienced his assurance, pray for others . . .").

---

4. Stott, *Epistles of John*, 185.

Appendix One

- What might be some sins that other believers commit that would cause us to intercede on their behalf, maybe even with greater effort?
- What is the significance of the word *see*?
    - *Must be certain*
    - *Must not simply be suspected or a doubtful matter*
- Define brother or sister:
    - *A fellow Christian in spiritual need*
        - *Pray for this person's restoration.*
        - *If the person dies, however, don't pray for the dead (1 Cor 5:1–10; 11:30).*
    - *Possibly a so-called brother: one who associates with believers but isn't one (1 Cor 5:11–13)*
        - *If he isn't apostate (2:18–19) or blaspheming the Holy Spirit (Matt 12:22–32), then pray for his soul.*
- Can you think of any sins that might be sins unto death, i.e., a sin that would lead to death or assure that one cannot enter the kingdom of heaven?

Possible Answers

- *Blasphemy of God, especially concerning the person and work of the Holy Spirit*
- *Someone uttering a curse against everything that Jesus is, did, and stands for*
- *Apostasy (rejection of the truths of Christ and the Christian faith)*
- *Heresy (is John possibly implying that the gnostic heretics are unworthy of prayer?)*

- **Verse 17:** "All wrongdoing is sin, but there is sin that does not lead to death."
    - Point: In distinguishing between the sin unto death and the sin not unto death, John is clear that he isn't trying to minimize sin. All sin is wrong—don't consider any sin lightly.

- ◆ What sins do we often tend to overlook or consider lightly in our lives?
- **Verse 18:** "We know that everyone who has been born of God does not keep on sinning, but he who was born of God protects him, and the evil one does not touch him."
  - Certainty 4: We know that no one born of God sins.
  - *Review from Lesson Seven (1 John 3:6):* what does the phrase "continue to sin" mean?
    - ◆ *Practice sin:*
      - *Plan—desire to be the god of our lives or of the moment*
      - *Enjoy—no conviction by the Holy Spirit; sin is an ongoing pleasure*
      - *Continue—no repentance of the sinful habit or practices*
  - What type of protection is John addressing? How does Christ protect us?

  Possible Answers

  - ◆ *His Spirit leads and guides us.*
  - ◆ *His Spirit gives us victory over sin.*
  - ◆ *His Spirit gives us strength to battle the evil one.*
  - Who is the evil one?

  Possible Answers

  - ◆ *Satan*
  - ◆ *The devil*
  - ◆ *The tempter*
  - ◆ *The accuser*
  - ◆ *The adversary*
  - ◆ *The lawless one*
  - ◆ *The serpent*
  - ◆ *The father of lies*
  - ◆ *The deceiver*

Appendix One

- Can the evil one touch (or harm) us?

  POSSIBLE ANSWERS

  - *I would suggest that the passage, in the context of the topic of assurance of eternal life, is stating that the devil cannot grab us out of God's hand (cf. John 10:28–30).*
  - *Meaning of touch: lay hold on—Satan can tempt and oppress us, but he cannot control, indwell, or possess us.*

- Can Satan make us slaves of sin once again?

  POSSIBLE ANSWER

  - *No, but he can oppress us, intimidate us, tempt us, try to make us afraid or worry. However, he can never possess us or enslave us to his diabolical will.*

- **Verse 19:** "We know that we are from God, and the whole world lies in the power of the evil one."
  - Certainty 5: We know that we are of God.
  - Certainty 6: We know that the whole world lies in the power of the evil one.
    - What does the word *whole* mean here (esp. in light of verse 18)?
      The unregenerate world—all unbelievers live under Satan's sway and dominion.

- **Verse 20:** "And we know that the Son of God has come and has given us understanding, so that we may know him who is true; and we are in him who is true, in his Son Jesus Christ. He is the true God and eternal life."
  - What is the understanding about which John is speaking? (Consider all of the messages throughout the entire book.)

    POSSIBLE ANSWERS

    - *That we can know God*
    - *That we can be in Christ*
    - *That our sins can be forgiven*

- - *That we can know truth*
  - *That we can know love*
  - *That we can seek purity*
  - *That we can have eternal life*
  - *That we can know Christ is God*
- **Verse 21:** "Little children, keep yourselves from idols."
  - Why do you think he closes with this final admonition?

  POSSIBLE ANSWERS

  - *As John considers the fact that the whole world lies in the power of the evil one (v. 19), he contemplates all the idols (material and spiritual) that surround the believers to whom he writes.*
  - *John knows that serving and living for God involves much competition in this life. All such competition is a form of dangerous idolatry.*
  - *John doesn't want all of the assurances that the believers have in Christ to cause them to relax in their walks of godliness.*

  - What is the tone of his final exhortation?
    - *No farewell, but calls them "little children"*
    - *Affectionate, although abrupt*
  - What are idols?
    Some scholarly answers:
    - *Anything which occupies the place of God*[5]
    - *Untrue mental images fashioned by false teachers*[6]
    - *A counterfeit, imitation, substitution, or false conception of God*[7]
  - What are idols we face in our world today?
  - How do we keep ourselves from idols in our lives?
  - Is there any one lesson in particular that you have gleaned from this study of 1 John?

5. Westcott, *Epistles of St. John*, 197.
6. Stott, *Epistles of John*, 197.
7. Bruce, *Epistles of John*, 128.

Appendix Two

Disciple Investing through Modified Inductive Bible Study

Working through the Book of Malachi

Malachi: Heart Attitudes
Modified Inductive Bible Study
Suggested Outline

Session	Topic	Passage
1	Introduction	
2	Questioning God's Love (Israel Questions God)	1:1–5
3	Polluted Worship by God's People	1:6–14
4	Dishonoring God's Name	2:1–9
5	Unfaithful Living (Disunity and Divorce)	2:10–16
6	Questioning God's Justice	2:17—3:6
7	Misuse of Money	3:7–12

Session	Topic	Passage
8	Serving God Is Useless	3:13–18
9	The Coming of Christ (God's Hope for the Future)	4:1–6

Introduction/Lesson One

Malachi

Questions for Discussion

NOTE TO LEADER

Answers to the questions below and suggestions for leading are provided for the leader, and those answers are in italics.

Fellowship and Introductions to One Another

Begin the small group study by building natural interaction among the participants and encouraging consistent attendance and involvement. There will be no homework or other assignments, but attending the Bible study and being involved in the discussion is crucial for the success of the group.

- Ask the following:
  - Name
  - Hometown
  - College major or present job
  - Something unique about oneself that others might not know
- Talk about the need for attendance.
- Plan at least one social get-together for the first two or three months.

Leader opens in prayer.

- Who is the author?

- Malachi—name means "my messenger"
- He is not mentioned anywhere else in Scripture.
- Why is he in the Bible? *His prophecy is the last prophecy of God to his people, and then God will cease to speak for four centuries.*
- When did he write/prophesy?
  - Approximately 433 BC as the best estimate; sometime after 458 BC
    - Edom was destroyed (1:3–5) in 587 BC or (most probably) 550–400 BC.
    - Some scholars believe that Edom assisted Babylon in the destruction of Jerusalem and of the temple, although the most likely scenario is that Edom exhorted the Babylonians to destroy Jerusalem (Ps 137:7).
    - Malachi parallels with Nehemiah, governor of Israel from 450 to 420 BC.
- To whom? To Israel, God's people collectively; these were the remnant and their descendants who had returned to the land many years earlier (1:1).
- Why?
  - Real life was tough; people were therefore questioning God's love.
    - The nation was experiencing drought (3:10).
    - The population of Israel was small (see the return of the remnants as recorded by Ezra and Nehemiah).
    - The nation was under Persian (governor) control; ultimately, they were slaves, having been previously disciplined by God for their rebellion and idolatry (1:8).
  - The nation of Israel was rebellious; therefore, they were experiencing a just judgment from God's hand.
    - Their worship had become nothing but formality, particularly for the spiritual leaders, the priests (1:6).
    - The people of God were filled with hypocrisy, and they were sluggish spiritually (2:17).

- The people of God were robbing God and not honoring or trusting him with their giving (3:8).
  - The people of God were practicing false worship (3:14).
  - Social injustice, immorality (3:5).
  - Their attitudes toward God had become cynical, insolent and what we might say, in colloquial terms, chippy. They were skeptical about the coming of the Messiah, which they thought would make life better for them. But they wondered "Where is he?" and "Is there really a God who acts on our behalf?" They were filled with unbelief, along with great apathy and disobedience.
  - They were hardened spiritually by their circumstances. Dr. Walter Kaiser calls their condition "practical atheism."[1]
- God still loves them; therefore, there is hope.
  - God's love is clearly affirmed (to these skeptics) in Mal 1:2.
  - Their hope is found in Mal 4:5–6.
- Characteristics
  - God addresses Israel in the first person forty times in fifty-five verses.
    - *What does this signify? God loves his people and wants to dialogue with them in such a way that they will return to him.*
    - Cf. Mal 1:2 (2x), 1:6.
  - The phrase "says the LORD of hosts" occurs twenty times in fifty-five verses.
  - God and his audience speak in questions (1:2, 6, 7, 8, 9, 13; 2:10, 14, 15, 17; 3:2, 7, 8, 13). "The most striking feature in the book is the running dialogue between a righteous God and a sarcastic, unfaithful people."[2]
  - God's majesty is described in the book (1:5, 11, 14; 2:2); he is indeed Master, Lord, and King

---

1. Kaiser, *Malachi*, 11.
2. Wolf, *Haggai and Malachi*, 59.

Lesson Two

Questioning God's Love (God's Love for Israel)

Malachi 1:1–5

Questions for Discussion

Hook

What is our natural response to God when we find ourselves in a difficult or problematic situation? What questions do we ask him? How do we respond when we think he has failed us?

- Read verses 1–5.
    - What is happening in Israel's heart?
    - How is God responding to Israel's questions?
    - What questions do you have about this passage?
- **Verse 1:** "The oracle of the word of the LORD to Israel by Malachi."
    - The phrase "word of the LORD" literally speaks of a "burden of the LORD."
    - How does the phrase "burden of the LORD" convey more than just the phrase "word of the LORD"?

        Possible Answer

        God's heart for the sin and brokenness of his people is conveyed by this phrase.

    - What does *burden* tell us about God's heart for his people and about God's character?

Working through the Book of Malachi

POSSIBLE ANSWER

God cares for us and loves his people, even when they are rebellious and disobedient.

- How should God's ability to be burdened over us affect our lives?

• **Verse 2:** "'I have loved you,' says the LORD. But you say, 'How have you loved us?' 'Is not Esau Jacob's brother?' declares the LORD. 'Yet I have loved Jacob . . .'"

- Does God still love Israel?
    - Why did God ever love Israel? (See Deut 7:6–8; Ezek 16:4–6.)
      Because of his pity and compassion—not because they were special or numerous—God chose them to be his special people and his treasure based solely upon his elective love.
    - What keeps us from loving those who have no natural attraction to us?
    - Why would we love someone whose response to us would bring us no personal benefit? What could motivate us to love in this context?
    - Can you give examples of unconditional love and service of this type?
- What does God's unconditional/elective love mean in your life? When and why do you need to remember it?
- Why is Israel asking, "How have you loved us?"

PROBABLE ANSWER

- *They do not and are not presently experiencing the blessing of God; thus they question his love for them.*
- *Their question is quite pointed toward God, including a certain air of skepticism. The express attitudes of distrust and disappointment with God demonstrate that the people want him only if they are blessed by him.*

Appendix Two

- When do we most question God's love for us?
- Who were Jacob/Esau?
  Twin brothers born to Isaac and Rebekah (see Gen 25:19–34). Jacob, the deceiver and the younger brother, becomes a patriarch or father of God's people, receiver of God's covenant promise to make a nation out of his seed, while Esau becomes one who does not value his firstborn status, which should have brought him the blessings of God's covenant promise.
- What two nations do Jacob and Esau become?
  Israel and Edom (make reference to a Bible map of ancient Israel)

• **Verses 3–4:** "'... but Esau I have hated. I have laid waste his hill country and left his heritage to jackals of the desert.' ⁴ If Edom says, 'We are shattered but we will rebuild the ruins,' the LORD of hosts says, 'They may build, but I will tear down, and they will be called "the wicked country," and "the people with whom the LORD is angry forever."'"

- How does God treat Jacob and Esau?
  Jacob is loved (v. 2) and Esau is hated (v. 3).
- How do you justify God's hatred for Esau/Edom?

  POSSIBLE ANSWER

  God's hatred is a rejection of an unholy people who are also the enemy of the people of God.

- How is God's hatred related to his anger?
- How is his hatred related to wickedness? (Cf. Pss 5:5–6; 11:5; 26:5; 106:40.)
- What do you think (or how do you feel) about God's holy hatred?
- Is God's election—or choosing—loving? Explain. (Cf. Rom 9:10–13.)
- Is God proving his love for Israel or his hatred of Edom in verses 3–4? How?
  - *Note*: Edom is destroyed by the Chaldeans in 587 BC or sometime thereafter (Jer 49:7–9; 25:9, 21).
- Do you think that there is ever any hope for Edom?

- What attribute is Edom expressing in verse 4?
  Pride and self-reliance.
- What is Edom saying about themselves?
  They can overcome adversity in their own strength.
- Why does God dislike Edom so much?
  They are full of themselves. Even from their origins in Esau, they have had no interest in the things of God.
- How are we like Edom?
- How might we exhibit pride in our lives when God chastens us?

- **Verse 5:** "Your own eyes shall see this, and you shall say, 'Great is the LORD beyond the border of Israel!'"
  - What does this response tell us about God?
    God will act, and he is sovereign over the nations. He can conquer the nations, and the nations will acknowledge his greatness. God is the God of nations and the whole earth.
  - Do you think that verse five is a response regarding God's love or God's hatred?
    - *Love—God's desire that his glory will spread beyond just Israel (fulfilled in the Great Commission through the church)*
    - *Hate—a demonstration of God's greatness—he has proved his grace through the destruction (hatred) of Edom and the salvation of (love for) Israel.*
  - What does this passage (1:1–5) tell us about God's love for his children (even when they are disobedient)?
  - What are the weaknesses (tough times) in your life when you wonder if God really loves you?
  - What reassures you that he does?
  - How is God's choosing/election a comfort to believers?

Lesson Three

Polluted Worship by God's People

Malachi 1:6–14

Questions for Discussion

Hook

What do you feel are the biggest expressions of hypocrisy in the church today? (*Note:* these answers could be endless depending upon the participants' experiences. Watch your time, and also do not let negative experiences predominate the discussion.)

- Read verses 6–14 (general overview).
    - What are the outward problems mentioned regarding Israel? (What are the correct things they are doing, but in an incorrect manner?)
        - *v. 7: In worship, they are presenting defiled food and despising the table.*
        - *v. 8: In worship, they are presenting blemished sacrifices.*
        - *v. 13: Prior to worship, they are involved in robbery/violence to obtain sacrifices.*
    - What are the inward (negative) attitudes described in this passage?
        - *v.6: No respect/honor of God or his name; despising God's name*
        - *v.13: They are bored and weary in worship, not engaged in serious worship of God; their worship isn't genuine.*
        - *v.14: They do not care about broken vows and presenting to God far less than their best.*

Working through the Book of Malachi

- How does this passage apply to those who are not priests/ministers, i.e., everyday Christians?

- **Verse 6:** "A son honors his father, and a servant his master. If then I am a father, where is my honor? And if I am a master, where is my fear? says the LORD of hosts to you, O priests, who despise my name. But you say, 'How have we despised your name?'"

    - How are the relationships between a son and a servant different? *Honor versus fear; love versus duty; natural, hereditary relationship versus unnatural*

    - What is the difference between a father and a master? How is God both?

    - What do you suppose is the difference between honoring and fearing the LORD? What are the similarities?

    - How do we demonstrate honor of the LORD? How do we demonstrate fear of the LORD? Give an illustration of each.

    - How do we demonstrate dishonor of or lack of fear of the LORD?

    - What do these priests indicate about themselves when they say, "How have we despised your name"? *They are either in denial about or are unaware of their own spiritual insensitivity to the things of the LORD.*

- **Verse 7:** "By offering polluted food upon my altar. But you say, 'How have we polluted you?' By saying that the LORD's table may be despised."

    - What was defiled about the food?
    Cf. vv. 8, 13.

    - What does this accusation say about their worship and their view of God?

Personal Application

- How do we struggle with corporate (group) worship (i.e., how do we, at times, find it personally dissatisfying or contemptible)?

Appendix Two

NOTES TO LEADER

Don't let an atmosphere of worship criticism or worship debates take over the discussion.

- How do we struggle with our private worship (personal devotions)?
- How do we make corporate worship meaningful (or more meaningful) Sunday after Sunday in our personal lives?
- What can we do to better prepare ourselves on a Saturday (day or evening), so that our hearts are ready and engaged for corporate local church worship on the LORD's Day?
- How do we make our private worship more meaningful without falling into fads, false mysticism, and pseudoprayer methods (the use of the labyrinth, mantra prayers, the Jesus prayer, contemplative prayer, etc.)?
- How does our view of God impact our worship of God, personally and corporately?

- **Verse 8:** "When you offer blind animals in sacrifice, is that not evil? And when you offer those that are lame or sick, is that not evil? Present that to your governor; will he accept you or show you favor? says the LORD of hosts."

  - Notice the relationship between the altar (worship) and the nature of God. What is God's (the LORD of host's) rationale for decrying the sacrifices of the people of Israel? *They would never give such poorly chosen, inferior, and substandard gifts to a respectable political leader.*
  - What does God say is evil in this verse? Why is it evil? Do we ever think of our worship as being actually evil? What would ever make our worship of God evil in his sight?
  - Who appears at fault for these bad sacrifices being presented—the people or the priests? *The priests, as leaders and quality control advocates, are probably the bigger problem. They are failing to rebuke the people, who are also at fault.*
    - Why do you think the priests are compromising?

Possible Answers

- *For the sake of growth*
- *To keep from being rejected as priests*
- *To maintain the routine or the status quo, etc.*

Contemporary Application

Where do we observe such compromise in our churches today?

- Is our own worship ever wrong? In what way(s)?
- What is God's feeling toward ungodly worship?

Possible Answers

- *It is unacceptable or worse.*
- *It is rejected.*
- *It is neither sincere nor honoring to him.*

- If unbelievers' worship is unacceptable to God, what would be the reasons we should invite non-Christians to a worship service?
- How is worship (giving of ourselves to God) costly (i.e., requiring sacrifice) to us personally? What sacrifices do we or should we do to make our worship of God more meaningful and sincere?
- How do we engage in genuine worship of the Lord?

Personal Application

How does doing all things to the glory of God impact our worship? How do we use our talents, training, gifts, resources, abilities, etc., to worship God?

- How does worship on Sunday morning (and/or evening) relate to worship in all of life (i.e., in everything we do)?

- **Verse 9:** "'And now entreat the favor of God, that he may be gracious to us. With such a gift from your hand, will he show favor to any of you?' says the LORD of hosts."
  - Why do they need to plead with God? When does God not hear our prayers? *When our prayers are self-centered and we are not*

Appendix Two

praying for the will of God in our lives; when we do not repent of known sin (Ps 66:18)

- Does God hear everybody's prayers all the time? *Because of his omniscience and omnipresence, he does hear all prayers, but he will answer (hear effectually) only prayers made through the mediation of Christ (1 Tim 2:5; Heb 2:14, 7:25).*

- Is there anything in this passage that might indicate that these people are believers?

- **Verse 10:** "Oh that there were one among you who would shut the doors, that you might not kindle fire on my altar in vain! I have no pleasure in you, says the LORD of hosts, and I will not accept an offering from your hand."

  - *Note:* Doors/gates = the temple, which is restored after the return from the great dispersion caused by the invasions of Assyria and Babylon

  - What might useless and/or displeasing worship look like in the church today?

  - What does this verse say about God's need for our worship? Why does God call us to worship him? Is worship unnecessary?

  - If our hearts aren't right or prepared for worship on the LORD's Day, why shouldn't we just stay home? How do we remedy this situation?

- **Verse 11:** "For from the rising of the sun to its setting my name will be great among the nations, and in every place incense will be offered to my name, and a pure offering. For my name will be great among the nations, says the LORD of hosts."

  - Note this positive statement: no matter how hopeless a situation might appear, the theme of hope occurs in all the prophets!

  - Why is this verse here? It looks out of place between verses 10 and 12. *God doesn't need Israel; the nations will one day offer him true worship.*

  - Are the words incense and offering to be interpreted literally? *The Israelites would understand the literal meaning, since incense accompanied Jewish temple sacrifice and offerings; but in regard to the future, the passage seems to emphasize that the nations will properly worship the living God, the LORD of hosts (but figuratively, not with literal incense), in a spirit of genuine worship.*

- What is God saying about his name (note: there are three mentions of the word *name* in one verse)?
- How does God make his name great?

POSSIBLE ANSWERS

- *He receives the glory due to his name and his being or character.*
- *Christ is lifted up to the nations.*
- *All the peoples of the earth will worship the one, true, and living God.*

- Is this speaking of a thousand-year reign of Christ on earth? Should it be taken:
   1. Literally, i.e., a literal thousand-year reign of Christ on earth, what is called the *premillennial* view?
   2. Spiritually, i.e., a spiritual kingdom, the *amillennial* view of a long period of spiritual warfare between God's goodness and Satan's evil?
   3. Symbolically, i.e., a long era of victory of the gospel on earth before the second coming of Christ, also known as the *postmillennial* view?

NOTE TO LEADER

Don't try to explain or discuss every detail of these three views. You will never finish the study, and simply asking this question could distract from the more important applications of the text.

- **Verses 12–13:** "But you profane it when you say that the LORD's table is polluted, and its fruit, that is, its food may be despised. ¹³ But you say, 'What a weariness this is,' and you snort at it, says the LORD of hosts. You bring what has been taken by violence or is lame or sick, and this you bring as your offering! Shall I accept that from your hand? says the LORD."
    - What are priests saying/doing in verses 12–13? *Shifting the blame. The problem is, the priests say, that the table and the food are not*

Appendix Two

meaningful to the people. They don't like their role, because no one really cares. They are tired of ministry.

- The priests are putting the blame on the people and the worship system. Is it possible for ministers to do this today? How?
- These priests are both bored with and weary of their duty/responsibility. How might this affect ministers today? What might they tire of and give up doing or give less effort toward, and why?
- How would this affect the average layperson in the church today? What would they tire of and give up doing or give less effort toward, and why?

Personal Application

What makes you weary/bored in the Christian life?

Contemporary Application

How do churches improperly attempt to keep their worship services and ministries from being boring?

General Application

Debate the following issue in today's worship: the entertainment or seeker-friendly church vs. the church of teaching, doctrine, and serious discipleship.

Practical Application

Why do we worship? What is the purpose of worship, and why do we at times become bored with it?

- Is boredom in worship our problem, the pastor's problem, the church's problem, or a combination of any or all of the above?
- According to the passage, the priests have what we might call loose standards. They are allowing the people to bring anything, including the substandard, for their sacrifices.
    - How does this relate to today's church? How are ministers loose in the church today? Can you think of any contemporary examples?

PRACTICAL APPLICATION

How do we (or churchgoers) feel . . .

- When worship goes longer than sixty to seventy minutes?
- When the minister reads a forty-verse chapter?
- The sermon goes more than forty-five minutes (as opposed to our involvement with sporting events, movie-watching, Facebook-viewing, social media engagement, etc.)?

- **Verse 14:** "Cursed be the cheat who has a male in his flock, and vows it, and yet sacrifices to the LORD what is blemished. For I am a great King, says the LORD of hosts, and my name will be feared among the nations."

  - What were the people doing in their worship of God? How were their vows ungodly?
  - How do we cheat God today, either in our personal lives or in the life of our churches?
  - How are we hypocritical in our own worship of God?
  - What does God say about himself in this verse? How does our worship reflect our knowledge of God's character? Vice versa?

Lesson Four

Dishonoring God's Name

Malachi 2:1–9

Questions for Discussion

Hook

At what point do you determine that a leader is no longer worth following or listening to? What is the primary issue that prevents you from respecting the leader?

- **Verses 1–2:** "And now, O priests, this command is for you. ²If you will not listen, if you will not take it to heart to give honor to my name, says the LORD of hosts, then I will send the curse upon you and I will curse your blessings. Indeed, I have already cursed them, because you do not lay it to heart."
    - How do you apply a passage written to priests (such as this one) to your own life?
    - What applications did/do you get from this passage? What does it (1) say? (2) mean? (3) mean to you?
    - What is the commandment/admonition contained in verse 2?
        - *To listen to God's rebuke*
        - *To give honor to God's name*
    - What is the bottom-line problem with the priests?
    - *They don't have the proper heart.*
    - Do you think it is worse for the priests/leaders not to have a heart for God than it is for the laypeople or the people in the pew not to have a heart for God? Why or why not?

- Why is God's name so important to him (think about how you feel when someone misstates or denigrates your own name)?

PossIBLE ANSWERS

- *His name represents his character.*
- *His name is to be revered, not mocked or disrespected.*
- *His name demands awe and respect.*

- How are they dishonoring God's name? (Cf. Exod 20:7; Num 6:22–26.)
- How might we dishonor God's name (what are the various ways our culture misuses God's name)?
- How does God respond to their false or lackluster hearts?
- How does God respond to our false hearts? Is it the same in both the Old Testament and the New Testament?
- What are God's judgments on the priests?
    - What are the blessings?
    We will assume crops, fields, and harvests, i.e., the livelihood of the nation/people living in an agrarian culture.
- How can the priests honor God's name? What do they need to change?

PossIBLE ANSWERS

- *They need to lead the people according to God's word.*
- *They must rebuke the people for their sinful and dishonoring sacrifices (see ch. 1).*

PERSONAL APPLICATION

How do we honor (and dishonor) God's name?

- How has God already cursed them? *He has probably diminished their crops.*
    - Do you think that God is being too harsh with the priests?

- **Verse 3:** "Behold, I will rebuke your offspring, and spread dung on your faces, the dung of your offerings, and you shall be taken away with it."
  - Who or what are their offspring/descendants?

    POSSIBLE ANSWERS
    - *Their children*
    - *Their children, i.e., sons in the priestly line*
    - *Their grain and crops*
    - *Their ministries*

  - How bad do we have to be to have God curse us like this? Would he even curse us like this?

    POSSIBLE ANSWER
    - *Some of God's anger might be based on the priestly responsibilities (greater accountability), the relinquishing of God's high standards, setting a poor example for the people, and being halfhearted for the things of God. Their position would require a higher responsibility and therefore a stricter judgment.*

  - Why does God use this refuse/dung metaphor? *It speaks of a most ignominious treatment. God will not only discipline them, but he will humiliate them, because they have dishonored his glory.*
  - What does God mean by taken away?
    - *To be swept like dung or removed from God's presence*
    - *To be mocked by other people, due to their rejection by God (refuse on their faces to be seen by others; like egg on your face)*
    - *Note: think about dung metaphors: flushing, scooping, and tossing away, removing the stench or smell.*
  - Discuss: is this a picture of God being vengeful or God being just? (Or are both related?)
  - How do you feel about God's harshness toward these religious leaders?

- **Verse 4:** "So shall you know that I have sent this command to you, that my covenant with Levi may stand, says the LORD of hosts."
  - What is a covenant? *A promise or an agreement between two parties.*
  - Who is Levi? *Levi is the head of the priestly line of Israel known as the Levites, the sons of Aaron. God is obviously speaking to and against the priests of Malachi's day. Cf. Num 3:6, 45; Num 18:1–7.*
- **Verse 5:** "My covenant with him was one of life and peace, and I gave them to him. It was a covenant of fear, and he feared me. He stood in awe of my name."
  - What did God promise the obedient priests? *Life and peace*
  - How do we evaluate life and peace today, i.e., how do we know we have life from, as well as peace with, God?
  - What does it look like when a person doesn't have life? What does it look like when a person doesn't have peace in his or her life?
  - How does revering God and standing in awe of him bring us life and peace?
- **Verse 6:** "True instruction was in his mouth, and no wrong was found on his lips. He walked with me in peace and uprightness, and he turned many from iniquity."
  - What are the characteristics of the godly priest/person, as mentioned in verse 6? *One who speaks truth, who has blameless speech, whose words honor God, who walks with God and does so in peace (the fruit of righteous living) and with integrity, who helps others to repent of the sins plaguing their lives.*
  - Why do we no longer respectfully call another person godly? What has happened to the concept of godliness in our culture? Whom do you think of as being godly; can you name anyone?
  - What do verses 6–7 tell us about the teaching of the Levites/priests as it should be?
    Truth, righteousness, peace-oriented, turning others from sin

Appendix Two

Contemporary Application

How/why do ministers compromise truth and righteousness in the church today?

Practical Application

What does it mean to walk with God?

Possible Answers

- We are walking in faith.
- We are fellowshipping with God and his people.
- We have assurance and security in God's promises and presence.
- We maintain confidence in God's loving work in our lives.
- We increase in intimacy with God through prayer and a growing relationship.
- We find grace and joy in our relationship with God.
- (Cf. Gen 5:21–24: "Enoch walked with God.")

- What does it mean to walk in peace and uprightness with God? What might that look like?

Personal Application

What disrupts one's walk with God?

- Why do we sometimes cease to walk with God (at least temporarily)?

- **Verse 7:** "For the lips of a priest should guard knowledge, and people should seek instruction from his mouth, for he is the messenger of the LORD of hosts."

  - What does it mean to guard knowledge?

Possible Answers

- To remain faithful to the Scriptures (certainly the Torah or the five books of Moses)
- To maintain biblical doctrines, especially, in this context, those that honor the LORD of hosts and his name

- *To promote truth in general and truth about God and how he reveals himself in particular*
- How is biblical knowledge disappearing from the church today?

  POSSIBLE ANSWERS
  - *Theological liberalism doubts the integrity, trustworthiness, and truth of God's word.*
  - *Preaching and teaching is compromised and either isn't based on the Scriptures or handles the word of God lightly.*
  - *Preachers read the Bible to their people but don't preach it.*
  - *Christian education in the local church is not emphasized as it was previously.*
  - *The church is producing biblically illiterate members and young people.*
- How much emphasis should there be on receiving instruction (i.e., seeking to be taught or being taught) in our walk with God? Is there a balance between being self-taught and learning from others? What might be the advantages of both? What might be the weaknesses of a believer who seeks truth in only one of these avenues, i.e., only being self-taught or only learning from the experts?

  CONTEMPORARY APPLICATION

  "Messenger of the LORD"—how much respect ought one give to an ordained minister or one called by God to speak/preach his word?

- **Verses 8–9:** "But you have turned aside from the way. You have caused many to stumble by your instruction. You have corrupted the covenant of Levi, says the LORD of hosts, ⁹and so I make you despised and abased before all the people, inasmuch as you do not keep my ways but show partiality in your instruction."
  - According to verses 8–9, how have these priests of Malachi's day failed the ideal? *They have caused the people to sin, mostly out of ignorance. They have failed in their responsibilities as spiritual leaders and teachers.*

Appendix Two

- What do you think it means to turn aside from the way? *To compromise the truth and their duty to maintain God's truth and the true worship of God.*
- How does poor instruction cause people to stumble in their daily walks of life and their relationship with God?
- Why do you think people continue to go to churches that have leaders who have compromised the biblical faith (i.e., liberal teachers, the lukewarm, or even unbelievers and skeptics), lost zeal for ministry, or shown partiality to others?

Possible Answers

- *They want their sinful lives to be affirmed; they don't want to be confronted for the wrong they are doing.*
- *They don't want to hear God's strong rebukes: "so says the LORD . . ."*
- *They are simply going through the motions or following the pattern that their parents gave them, and it is without real meaning.*
- *They see the church as a network for their business.*
- *They see the church as a place of support, relationships, and maybe fun—a wholesome social outlet.*
- *They think that going to church and/or doing good will make up for their disobedience and the guilt it incurs.*
- *They see the church as an avenue for social justice and activism, contributing to the improvement of their community*

Lesson Five

Unfaithful Living (Disunity and Divorce)

Malachi 2:10–16

Questions for Discussion

Hook

The divorce rate in America in 1910 was 1/10. In 1973, it was approximately 5/10 and continues to be close to that number in the early twenty-first century (39 percent), despite cohabitation increasing dramatically as well. What do you think made the difference between 1910 and today's marriages? What motivates divorce? What ideals do you cling to in order to be encouraged in maintaining marital vows?

- **Read verses 7–16.**
    - Do you see any transition or relationship between 2:1–9 and 2:10–16? Why does the passage seem to change so abruptly?

    Possible Answers

    - *The ungodliness of the priests and their lackadaisical teaching may have led to unfaithful marriages. This is certainly one way that the priests have made the people stumble.*
    - *Malachi might be building the parallel between bad teaching and bad marriages (living).*
    - *Malachi might be rather angry about the failures of the priests as he speaks to them as a prophet for God.*

- **Verse 10:** "Have we not all one Father? Has not one God created us? Why then are we faithless to one another, profaning the covenant of our fathers?"

Appendix Two

- Who is the father about whom Malachi is speaking?

    POSSIBLE ANSWERS

    - *Some think it is either Abraham, as the original patriarch, or Jacob, as he is mentioned frequently in the book of Malachi.*
    - *But from the context, it appears that the one father is God (Yahweh) himself.*

- What is the problem contained in this verse? *The problem is disunity, particularly the issue of dealing negatively with others, as it is contrary to God's design and plan for his people.*
- How is this concept of unity related to the problem of divorce?

    PROBABLE ANSWER

    - *Disunity becomes a cultural norm and influences all of life.*
    - *Disunity creates fragmented relationships among people (consider various national political divisions) and thus causes a spirit of fighting instead of reconciliation.*
    - *Disunity creates and fosters distrust among people.*
    - *Disunity tends toward accusation and leads to a polarization of the other person's views. These two attitudes and postures cause hatred.*

- Who are the we and us mentioned in the verse? *The most likely answer is that these pronouns are speaking of and to Israel (the people of God), not necessarily to all people everywhere.*
- What covenant were they breaking?
  God's promise to Abraham, Isaac, and Jacob to be their God and theirs to be God's people (cf. Gen 12:1–3, Abraham; Gen 26:1–5, Isaac; Gen 28:10–15, Jacob).

- **Verse 11:** "Judah has been faithless, and abomination has been committed in Israel and in Jerusalem. For Judah has profaned the sanctuary of the LORD, which he loves, and has married the daughter of a foreign god."

- How is Israel/Judah breaking the covenant? *They are committing spiritual adultery, which is considered to be adultery before the sight of the LORD.*

PERSONAL APPLICATION

How does our personal failure or disobedience affect the body of Christ (the group or your church)? Can you cite specific examples without using names?

- Why do you think he adds the phrase "and in Jerusalem?" *Jerusalem is the holy city, the city of David, the city of Zion representing God's holy presence. Even it has been desecrated! And not only it, but the temple—God's sanctuary—has been desecrated.*

- What does verse 11 tell us about God's view of marriage?
Note: it is always assumed in Israel that marriage is properly only between a man and a woman. Anything else would require excommunication from the nation, i.e., from the theocracy/the people of God.

- How has God's sanctuary been profaned (desecrated)?
They have become involved in mixed marriages with people who worship foreign gods. The people of the LORD (Yahweh) have united themselves with idols (false gods) through unholy marriages.
    ◆ Cf. Ezra 9:1–3; Neh 10:30, 13:23–29; 1 Cor 6:15–16.

PERSONAL APPLICATION

How do you know when God wants you to marry a particular person? What criteria should a Christian consider? How do a non-Christian's criteria differ, if any, from the Christian's, when it comes to considering the marital relationship?

- *Note:* the following questions could create a lot of discussion (take a considerable amount of time) and also could create a lot of potential volatility. Beware of causing disunity while discussing the problem of disunity!

- What do you think of the statement "A Christian may marry any (professing) Christian"?

Appendix Two

- What do you think of the statement "A Christian can never marry an obvious or a seemingly non-Christian person"?
- What do you think of the statement "A Christian must never date a non-Christian"?
- When is a Christian out of God's will in the act of marriage?

- **Verse 12:** "May the LORD cut off from the tents of Jacob any descendant of the man who does this, who brings an offering to the LORD of hosts!"

  > **NOTE TO LEADER**
  >
  > Some versions translate the verse, "As for the man who does this, may the LORD cut off from the tents of Jacob everyone who awakes and answers, or who presents an offering to the LORD of hosts" (NASB). What does awakes and answers mean? *This is an obscure phrase, an idiom, and is not clear. It could mean anyone who responds in this way. It could also mean everyone, both teacher and student, or everyone, both adult and child. It is uncertain, but the thrust is that all who bring idolatry into marriage should be cut off.*

  - In the phrase "the man who does this," what is *this*? *Context: verse 11 (marries someone following a foreign God)*
  - Is Malachi addressing all the people or the Levites or both? *Probably anyone who is a member of the nation of Israel, the people of God*
  - What is the meaning of tents of Jacob? *The people of Israel, humbly called into covenant as was the undeserving patriarch, Jacob; ultimately, the man who does this should be cut off from Israel, the conduit of redemption and the covenant people*
  - Why do you think that the LORD of hosts is so harsh about this sin? Why would excommunication (being cast out of the people of God) be the consequence for this sin (coming to worship God while violating his will about marrying only those who truly believe in him)?

- **Verses 13–14:** "And this second thing you do. You cover the LORD's altar with tears, with weeping and groaning because he no longer regards the offering or accepts it with favor from your hand. [14] But you say, 'Why does he not?' Because the LORD was witness between you and the wife of your youth, to whom you have been faithless, though she is your companion and your wife by covenant."

- About whose tears do you think he is speaking, the wives or the divorcing husbands?
    - If the wives, why are they weeping? *They are expressing sorrow for their loss and the abuse they have received through divorce.*
    - If husbands, what are they doing? *Possibly they are trying to convince God that they are sorry for their actions, wishing to appease him, although they are still in their sin of divorce.*

PERSONAL APPLICATION

How do we become insensitive to sin in our lives? How can we become insensitive to a sin of the magnitude of divorce, when potentially multiple relationships are damaged or destroyed? (*Note*: Divorce is an extremely painful topic and very common, so handle this discussion with great sensitivity.)

- According to verse 14, why is God not listening? *God is not blessing them, because he sees their sins against their wives.*

CONTEMPORARY APPLICATION

How does love move from covenant promises (vows) and commitments of faithfulness, made to each other, to the point of dealing treacherously with another (in this case, by the husbands)?

- Does the type of marriage ceremony a person plans have anything to do with that person's view of marriage itself? Why or why not? *The issue here is whether or not the ceremony dignifies the concept of marriage or trivializes it.*
- What is verse 14 saying about marriage and marital relationships?

POSSIBLE ANSWERS

- *It is a commitment before God.*
- *It is companionship.*
- *It is a heartfelt covenant: it involves vows and promises to one's first choice and first love.*

Appendix Two

- ♦ *Your partnership is built upon harmony, commitment, faithfulness, and communication.*

- **Verses 15–16:** "Did he not make them one, with a portion of the Spirit in their union? And what was the one God seeking? Godly offspring. So guard yourselves in your spirit, and let none of you be faithless to the wife of your youth. ¹⁶'For the man who does not love his wife but divorces her, says the LORD, the God of Israel, covers his garment with violence, says the LORD of hosts. So guard yourselves in your spirit, and do not be faithless.'"

  - These verses (15–16) are not an easy explanation of the problem mentioned in verses 13–14, but what do you think Malachi is saying in verse 15?
  - About whom is he speaking?

  POSSIBLE ANSWERS

  - ♦ *Abraham, who went to Hagar when Sarah could not have children (although this was not a divorce, it did subvert the intent of a marriage bond)*
  - ♦ *Most likely answer: the* one *is God, who created marriage and gave Adam one wife in order to have godly offspring. (God did not give Adam more than one wife, even though he sought the offspring that would glorify him. Imagine the unthinkable scenario of Adam rejecting his wife.)*

  - Why has marriage declined so much as an institution in our society? Why is there so much divorce (and living together without or prior to marriage) today?
  - How is divorce often justified?
  - How is divorce related to a culture of faithlessness?
  - What does "covers his garment with violence" mean? *The wedding garment with which a man would cover his wife (claiming her as his wife) symbolized that he would provide for her and protect her (the opposite of violence). See Ruth 3:8–9; Deut 22:30.*

- Does God ever allow divorce in certain circumstances?
  - *See Matt 5:31–32; 19:1–9 (adultery, breaking the oneness bond).*
  - *See also 1 Cor 7:11–15 (desertion, irreparable breaking of the oneness bond).*

Lesson Six

Questioning God's Justice

Malachi 2:17—3:6

Questions for Discussion

Hook

When things go wrong in our lives, what is our natural response to God (assuming that we believe in him)? What about when our plans get fouled up and others' plans go well?

- **Verse 17:** "You have wearied the LORD with your words. But you say, 'How have we wearied him?' By saying, 'Everyone who does evil is good in the sight of the LORD, and he delights in them.' Or by asking, 'Where is the God of justice?'"
  - What is the attitude of those speaking after they hear Malachi tell them that they are wearying the LORD?

    POSSIBLE ANSWERS
    - *Indifference*
    - *Sarcasm*
    - *Denial*
    - *Ignorance*

  - Of the three phrases (below) used to describe how they have wearied God, which do you think impugns God's character the most? Why?
    - Everyone who does evil is good in the sight of the Lord.
    - He delights in them.

WORKING THROUGH THE BOOK OF MALACHI

- Where is the God of justice?

PERSONAL APPLICATION

Give a practical everyday example of others succeeding and you failing.

POSSIBLE ANSWERS/SCENARIOS

- *Cheating on exams and getting good grades*
- *Loafing on the job, yet getting a raise*
- *Cheating on taxes, but having a nicer home/car*
- *Flirting with the boss and yet getting the promotion*
- *Speeding past you at 90 mph, but you get stopped by the police*

- Does God grow weary with us? Is not his patience infinite? When does his patience run out? *God does have infinite patience, but he also expects our obedience. When we rebel at our own peril and the peril of others, he may very well run out of patience with us. His discipline (for our good) or his justice (for his glory) may be the reasons behind what we would call, humanly speaking, God's weariness.*

- Compare Israel to the other nations: what were the people expecting God to do for them (i.e., for Israel) based on their return to Jerusalem/the promised land?

POSSIBLE ANSWERS

- *Liberating Israel*
- *Bringing the Messiah to them (a legitimate hope)*
- *Making them great again (nostalgia for the days of Kings David and Solomon)*
- *Conquering their enemies*

- In their own minds, what are they doing right, so as to gain God's favor?

POSSIBLE ANSWERS

- *Attending temple worship*

- *Praying*
- *Giving to God*
- *Weeping over their divorces (possibly)*
  - How do we change a complaining spirit into a joyful spirit?

  POSSIBLE ANSWERS
  - *Walk by faith.*
  - *Practice waiting on God (patience).*
  - *Find things in your life for which to be grateful.*
  - Is "Where is the God of justice?" a legitimate, honest question?
    - Why is it not legitimate for the people of Israel to ask?
    - Why do you think that God hadn't judged the evil nations (thus leaving Israel in slavery and vulnerability)?

- Read Mal 3:1–5.
  - Are these verses the answer to the question of verse 17?
- **Verse 1:** "Behold, I send my messenger, and he will prepare the way before me. And the Lord whom you seek will suddenly come to his temple; and the messenger of the covenant in whom you delight, behold, he is coming, says the LORD of hosts."
  - Who is speaking in 3:1? *The LORD of hosts.*
  - About whom is he speaking?
    - *A forerunner—e.g., when a king comes to town, people/servants go ahead and they make necessary preparation for his stay or visit.*
    - *Cf. John 1:21–23. Do you think this is speaking of John the Baptist preparing the way for Jesus? See also Matt 11:10–14; Luke 1:15–17; Luke 7:27.*
  - How is the messenger to prepare the way? *Spiritual housecleaning, i.e., helping people to think through their need for the Messiah*
    - How is John the Baptist's ministry on behalf of Christ similar to our ministry on behalf of Christ today? *Topic: evangelism*

- How did Christ suddenly come? *Ultimately, he appeared when unexpected, and he also appears almost immediately after the beginning of the public preaching of John the Baptist*
  - What does *suddenly* usually denote? *Often disaster and surprise—cf. 2 Pet 3:10.*
  - *Note:* there was a four hundred-year delay between Malachi's prophecy and Christ's first coming. Christ's coming is indeed sudden but not quick.
  - Why does the LORD come to the temple? *It is the place of sacrifice and the symbol of God's presence (from the past).*
  - Why is he called the messenger of the covenant? *See Gen 3:15 and the promise of the coming Messiah to Adam and Eve, also the new covenant proclaimed by Jeremiah; cf. Jer 31:31–34; 33:1–9.*

- **Verse 2:** "But who can endure the day of his coming, and who can stand when he appears? For he is like a refiner's fire and like fullers' soap."
  - What does it mean to refine something? *To purify or remove unwanted elements in it*
  - How was God going to refine them? *Both John the Baptist and Christ himself will call the nation of Israel to repentance. The people of Israel, including their leaders, have impure hearts. They don't love God.*
  - How does God refine us?
  - Why fuller's soap? What is it? *Fuller soap is a soap used to cleanse and whiten stained garments.*
  - Are there two different trials or simply one thought in these two metaphors—fire and soap? What do you see as the differences (and similarities) between both metaphors?

- **Verses 3–4:** "He will sit as a refiner and purifier of silver, and he will purify the sons of Levi and refine them like gold and silver, and they will bring offerings in righteousness to the LORD. ⁴Then the offering of Judah and Jerusalem will be pleasing to the LORD as in the days of old and as in former years."
  - *Note:* A refiner (or smelter) is finished with his task when the silver becomes a liquid mirror in which the refiner's image is reflected.

Appendix Two

- Why the sons of Levi? *As spiritual leaders, the priests were failing miserably and would be held accountable by the LORD; see Jas 3:1ff.*
- Was the priesthood (the sons of Levi) actually refined at this time? *Apparently not. Israel is judged for the next four hundred years by God's silence to them.*
- (*Note:* this is a heavy question) Do we take these verses literally, expecting a new Jerusalem, as well as a literal kingdom of God on earth? Or do we take them spiritually, speaking of a coming spiritual kingdom of God on earth? Explain your answer.
- How does our personal sanctification (v. 3) relate to our worship of the LORD (v. 4)? *Purity of life brings pleasure to the LORD and helps us to properly worship him. Sin inhibits proper worship of God.*

- **Verse 5:** "Then I will draw near to you for judgment. I will be a swift witness against the sorcerers, against the adulterers, against those who swear falsely, against those who oppress the hired worker in his wages, the widow and the fatherless, against those who thrust aside the sojourner, and do not fear me, says the LORD of hosts."
  - When is *then*?

  Possible Answers

  - *Christ's first coming, his rejection, and the ensuing fall of Jerusalem in AD 70 (destroyed by Rome).*
  - *Christ's second coming and the final judgment.*
  - *This is simply a general description that God ultimately will judge sin, answering the unbelief of Mal 2:17.*

  - List and count or number the sins mentioned in verse 5.
  - Why this list and not the sins they were committing in their false worship?

  Probable Answer

  He is addressing explicit, specific commandment breakers and those sins that clearly demonstrate a cold, unjust heart. The ultimate issue is that they do not fear the LORD.

- Is there an order, a logic, or a reasonable purpose behind the way this list is created?
- **Verse 6:** "For I the LORD do not change; therefore you, O children of Jacob, are not consumed."
  - How does God's immutability (he does not change) relate to:
    - Their not being consumed?
    - His being just (cf. Mal 2:17)?

Personal Application

How does reflecting upon God's immutability comfort us? *After looking at the list of sins to be judged, it is quite astonishing that God does wait to consume his radically disobedient children. We call this God's grace, and, indeed, it demonstrates his patience for recalcitrant, rebellious people. We, too, receive God's wonderful grace and kindness, and it should lead us to repentance, as well as to humble worship.*

Lesson Seven

Misuse of Money

Malachi 3:7–12

Questions for Discussion

Hook

Are Christians today required to tithe (i.e., give 10 percent of their earnings/income)? If not, what are the other options? (Cf. Abraham in Gen 14:20; Lev 27:30; Num 18:26–28; 2 Cor 8:1–15; 9:5–11.)

- **Verse 7:** "From the days of your fathers you have turned aside from my statutes and have not kept them. Return to me, and I will return to you, says the LORD of hosts. But you say, 'How shall we return?'"
  - Who is God speaking about when he mentions "your fathers"? *Possibly the people of Israel during the wilderness wanderings hundreds of years earlier in Israel's history. Certainly their disobedience began after Mount Sinai, when they received the Ten Commandments (God's statutes).*
  - Had there ever been a time when Israel as a nation had obeyed God? *(Discuss or trace their history as time allows; see Neh 9. Caution: this is an exhaustive study in itself.)*
  - What does verse 7 tell us about the character of God?
  - In what ways do believers today, or the twenty-first century church, need to return to God?
  - What is the attitude of the listeners displayed in verse 7? (*Note:* Remember the description of their attitudes as mentioned in the first lesson [Introduction] and in the General Overview for Mal 1:6–14.)

- **Verse 8:** "Will man rob God? Yet you are robbing me. But you say, 'How have we robbed you?' In your tithes and contributions."
  - What is the attitude of the respondents (those accused) displayed in verse 8? *Doubt, resentment, incredulity, taking offense (which is the attitude that most people demonstrate when asked about their finances and giving to God).*
  - Do you think this robbery is greater or of more concern than the other problems already mentioned in the book (cf. Mal 3:5)?
  - What is the difference between tithes *(10 percent)* and offerings *(voluntary gifts/portions of animals for priests)?*
  - If God ultimately owns all things, how can we rob him?
- **Verse 9:** "You are cursed with a curse, for you are robbing me, the whole nation of you."
  - What is the curse? *Judgment for trying to cheat God.*
  - Are there any parallels between Israel's sin/curse and living the Christian life today?
- **Verse 10:** "Bring the full tithe into the storehouse, that there may be food in my house. And thereby put me to the test, says the LORD of hosts, if I will not open the windows of heaven for you and pour down for you a blessing until there is no more need."
  - Why do most people, including seemingly committed Christians, fail to tithe?
  - What if you have little to no income—how can you tithe? *One option is to use "faith promise giving," a method in which you pray to and trust God to actually provide the income that you do not have. Then you give the promised income to God. The Scriptures do not clearly teach this method, but it does involve a faith that God loves to see in his children. You should also endeavor to give something of the little that you have, trusting God to take care of you.*
  - What do you think about a person tithing a gift (of money) received from another person?
  - What was the purpose of the tithe? *To pay the Levites for service and to take care of their needs.*

- What is the purpose of the tithe and/or giving to your church today?
- Why didn't the Israelites give more money (sacrificially)? Why don't we give more money (sacrificially)?
- What is the storehouse? *The treasury of the temple of the LORD (literally) and the place of God's blessing (figuratively).*
- What is your opinion about tithing only to the local church?
- What else do we tithe besides money?

  POSSIBLE ANSWERS
  - *Time*
  - *Talents*
  - *Spiritual gifts*
  - *Service*
  - *Self—focus upon ministry and giving one's energies to ministry*
- What improper attitudes can accompany our giving (tithing or not) even when we do give?
- What is God promising for Israel (in v. 10)? *He will give them—or pour out—blessings beyond their imaginations.*
- How would you expect/evaluate this God-given blessing in your life?
- Have you ever been blessed this much by God? (Cf. Eph 3:20.)
- What do you think about giving up almost everything you have/own/possess, so that you can expect a blessing?

• **Verse 11:** "I will rebuke the devourer for you, so that it will not destroy the fruits of your soil, and your vine in the field shall not fail to bear, says the LORD of hosts."

  - What is God's promise for Israel (in v. 11)? *He will take care of their crops if only they will trust and honor Him.*
  - Are there any parallels to the Christian life today in this promise?
  - How might this be used (inappropriately) as a health, wealth, and prosperity promise from God?

- **Verse 12:** "Then all nations will call you blessed, for you will be a land of delight, says the LORD of hosts."
  - What is God promising in this verse?
  - Was this promise ever fulfilled? *Ultimately, yes, through Christ, who comes to Israel to become the final sacrifice for the sins of the world (the nations).*
  - If God knows they will not eventually repent, is the promise legitimate?

Lesson Eight

Serving God Is Useless

Malachi 3:13–18

Questions for Discussion

Hook

What are some things in life that make believers wonder if it is worth being a Christian?

- **Read Mal 3:13–15.**
    - How do verses 13–15 relate to the previous section (vv. 10–12)?
    - What is the main point of verses 13–15?
- **Verse 13:** "Your words have been hard against me, says the LORD. But you say, 'How have we spoken against you?'"
    - What is the attitude God's people are displaying? Do you think it is the same as that which they previously expressed when they questioned God? *Cynical, insolent, incredulous, suspicious, possibly complaining*
    - What does verse 13 tell us about God's knowledge and his heart? *He grieves over our rebellion and obstinance and especially our lack of faith and trust and our obvious shallow love for him.*
- **Verse 14:** "You have said, 'It is vain to serve God. What is the profit of our keeping his charge or of walking as in mourning before the LORD of hosts?'"
    - Why do we sometimes feel like it is futile to serve God?
    - What keeps us from saying to ourselves and others, "It is futile to serve God"?

- Could you serve God if there were no blessings/reward?
  - (E.g., Isaiah, serving for fifty years with little fruit [Isa 6:8–13], or trying to reach unresponsive unbelievers in North Africa, or trying to change an unresponsive church in North America, or being imprisoned for twenty years in a country of persecution.)
  - How would you do this?—i.e., what would keep you motivated to serve God while experiencing little apparent response from those you are reaching or receiving very little encouragement in your work?
- What evil/harsh things are they saying about God? *He doesn't help us. He doesn't benefit us. We mourn, fast, and feel sad, but he doesn't appear to notice.*
- What do you think that they expect from God as they carry out his requirements? *Their crops will flourish. They might conquer their enemies. They might feel more secure.*
- What is their attitude toward living the Christian life? *It is worthless living for God; we obey, but it doesn't pay off (see Ps 73:1–3, 12–15).*

PERSONAL APPLICATION

How do we sometimes do this (obey for the sake of God's blessing) in our walks with the LORD?

- What are some ways believers treat God like he is a lucky rabbit's foot?
- What are some ways we attempt to manipulate God in order to get our own way?

- How were they going about like mourners? *They were wearing sackcloth, had darkened faces; they were fasting, with apparent concern for the nation, but that fasting wasn't genuine; it was hypocritical.*

PERSONAL APPLICATION

Discuss genuine fasting—the power of fasting, reasons for fasting, God's response to fasting, etc. (*Note:* this could be an entire Bible study/discussion in itself.)

- ◆ Why should believers fast today?
  - ▪ What do you think about believers questioning, or complaining to, God? (See Ps 73:12–14.)
- **Verse 15:** "And now we call the arrogant blessed. Evildoers not only prosper but they put God to the test and they escape."
  - ▪ How are the evil described?
  - ▪ What is their supposed reward?
  - ▪ What are these statements saying (wrongly) about God's character? *He allows evil, he doesn't judge arrogance, he lets the ungodly off the hook, they get away with their sin. Worse yet, God blesses them (and not us).*
- **Verse 16:** "Then those who feared the LORD spoke with one another. The LORD paid attention and heard them, and a book of remembrance was written before him of those who feared the LORD and esteemed his name."
  - ▪ What is different about verse 16 as compared to verses 13–15? *This verse must be speaking of the remnant of believers.*
  - ▪ How are the godly described? *They fear the LORD (mentioned twice) and they esteem his name.*
  - ▪ Define fear of the LORD. *Reverence, awe, respect, and a sense of humbled trembling before the almighty God of the universe. This is no ordinary fear.*
  - ▪ How does God respond to the godly? *He gives attention to their prayers, hears their prayers, and remembers their requests.*
  - ▪ What do you think is the meaning of "spoke with one another"? *Despite their circumstances, those who fear the LORD remain faithful and encourage one another to continue walking with and appealing to God, even if their prayers are not immediately answered.*
  - ▪ What do you think the book of remembrance is? *This is a culturally relevant phrase/concept. Persian kings would write down those deserving merits for future reward. (Cf. Ps 56:8).*
  - ▪ Why mention "esteemed his name"? Where was this mentioned previously? (Cf. Mal 1:6).

- **Verse 17:** "They shall be mine, says the LORD of hosts, in the day when I make up my treasured possession, and I will spare them as a man spares his son who serves him."
  - What is the day? *Probably the day of judgment and salvation*
  - What is God going to do in that day?
  - How does this answer the harsh things said about God? *He remembers his own in the time of judgment and is merciful (he will spare them). He loves the faithful, those who trust in him.*
  - What is the meaning of mine? *Adoption. God possesses them as his own; they will be brought into God's family.*
  - What is the meaning of treasured possession?
    - Do you have any treasured possessions? How do you feel about them?
    - What does this say about God's attitude toward us? *See Deut 7:6.*
    - *See the references in the New Testament with a similar meaning: Titus 2:14; 1 Pet 2:9.*
  - What is the meaning of spare? *Treat them with mercy, in contrast to the wicked*
- **Verse 18:** "Then once more you shall see the distinction between the righteous and the wicked, between one who serves God and one who does not serve him."
  - What is the distinction between righteous/wicked from now until the day of judgment?
  - Why do we look forward to this day—the day of judgment? Why do we ignore it?
  - How does the coming day of judgment impact the statement "It is vain to serve God. What is the profit of our keeping his charge or of walking as in mourning before the LORD of hosts?"

Lesson Nine

The Coming of Christ

(God's Hope for the Future)

Malachi 4:1–6

Questions for Discussion

Hook

Could Christ return tomorrow (or today)? Why do you think so, or why not?

- **Verse 1:** "For behold, the day is coming, burning like an oven, when all the arrogant and all evildoers will be stubble. The day that is coming shall set them ablaze, says the LORD of hosts, so that it will leave them neither root nor branch."
- **Review Mal 3:13–18.** How are these verses related to Mal 4:1?
    - What is the day? (It is used four times in the final eight verses of the book: 3:17; 4:1; 4:3; 4:5.)
        - *A future but final day in which the LORD will "destroy the whole earth" (Isa 13:5)*[3]
    - When is the day? *Probably the final day of judgment.*
    - What will this day reveal, as we reference the context in 3:18?
    - What does this verse tell us about God's character? *He is a judge who will be merciless to all evildoers.*
    - What does burning like a furnace signify? Compare it to open fires. *The intensity of the heat, destroying quickly and completely*

---

3. See Kaiser, *Malachi*, 102.

- Is this concept speaking of the annihilation (complete destruction of the souls) of the wicked? (See 2 Thess 1:6–9; God's judgment will bring eternal or everlasting banishment from the presence of the Lord.)
- Discuss the nature of hell (*Note:* this is an entire Bible study in itself).
- What is the significance of the mention of root and branch? *Complete destruction. Nothing will be spared or left remaining. Think about killing weeds in your yard. You have to dig them out completely to destroy them.*

- **Verse 2:** "But for you who fear my name, the sun of righteousness shall rise with healing in its wings. You shall go out leaping like calves from the stall."
  - Who or what is the sun of righteousness? *Most probably it is symbolic of Jesus (cf. 3:1; the messenger in this verse appears to be a reference to John the Baptist, the forerunner of Jesus).*
  - What thoughts about life and the future does the concept of the rising of the sun bring to mind? *Hope, a new day, life, brightness*
  - What is the meaning of healing? *Victory or vindication; speaks of salvation, glorification, and overcoming the pains of sin*
  - What is the meaning of wings? *Symbolically, flying conveys vigor and life (in this case, the sun is rising after a long winter of debilitating sin—four hundred years of God's silence—which will end with the coming of John the Baptist and God's Son, Jesus).*
  - What is the meaning of calves skipping? *Freedom and release, joy; for calves, this phrase often applies to their release after a long winter in the barns and stalls. (Note: You can find videos of this online. They are invigorating!)*
    - From what are the readers/listeners being freed?

Personal Application

How does Christ free us? How is living in the fear of the LORD freeing to us?

Appendix Two

- **Verse 3:** "And you shall tread down the wicked, for they will be ashes under the soles of your feet, on the day when I act, says the LORD of hosts."
  - What do you think this verse means or is talking about? (See Rom 16:20: "The God of peace will soon crush Satan under your feet." This phrase is spoken to believers. Also, see 1 Cor 6:2: "Or do you not know that the saints will judge the world?")
  - Is this an ugly picture or a victorious picture?
  - Can you imagine doing this to your spiritually lost loved ones? *It is a bit unimaginable. Of course, they have often considered you to be a fool for believing in and following Christ.*
  - How or why could it make sense? *Ultimately, God's judgment is for his own glory, and he vindicates his people who have suffered for following him and being associated with his name.*
  - What is God's point in this verse, considering the context of this book? *Ultimate vindication of God's glory will come even if his own people (Israel) are skeptical that he will ever do anything on their behalf. As disobedient as they might be in the day of Malachi, God will do good for his people and prevail (see 3:17–18 and Rom 16:20).*
  - Why the word ashes? *They will be utterly destroyed, as would be the case in the burning furnace.*
- **Verse 4:** "Remember the law of my servant Moses, the statutes and rules that I commanded him at Horeb for all Israel."
  - Why this shift in thought (from vindication and judgment to the law of Moses)? *To avoid God's judgment, the people need to repent. Moses's law has been completely disregarded by the ungodly priests. Don't follow them. Look to the law of Moses as your guide for holy living. Fear of and reverence for God will prevent God's judgment.*
  - To whom is God speaking, and what do you think is his purpose for bringing up the law of Moses?
  - How does the law of God relate to the Christian today? *It reflects God's holiness and is his holy standard. We are no longer condemned by it, because Christ took the penalty of the law on himself and on our behalf. There are three uses of the law: 1. To convict of sin and*

- What are the glorious attributes of God that are reflected in his law? *Holiness, goodness, and righteousness*
- What is the believer's relationship to the law? Are believers no longer under God's law?
- How is law related to grace? (*Note:* this is a big question and could require a good bit of time explaining the law/grace tension in the Christian life.)

- **Verse 5:** "Behold, I will send you Elijah the prophet before the great and awesome day of the LORD comes."
    - What is the relationship of verse 4 to verse 5? Is there any continuity? *Both the law and the prophets attest to the coming of the day of the LORD. Also, Moses and Elijah are symbolic of the entire Old Testament. Jesus not only fulfills the law (Moses), but he also fulfills prophecy (Elijah symbolizes all the great prophets of the Old Testament).*
    - How are verses 3:1 and 4:5 related? What are the similarities between the two?
    - Is the day spoken of in verse 5 describing the time before Jesus's first coming or Jesus's second coming? (*Note: this is a difficult question to answer, but the coming of "the great and awesome day of the LORD" sounds like it describes Christ's second coming in glory.*)
    - If this isn't speaking of the Old Testament prophet Elijah, why does God use the name Elijah? Why would God not use the names David, Abraham, Moses, Isaiah, etc.? What does Elijah represent in the Old Testament?
        - *Elijah is the head of the prophetic order.*
        - *Walter Kaiser states that a prophet is a forth teller, always preaching Christ from his word, declaring the second coming (v. 5) and restoring families (v. 6), the strength of the church.*[4]
        - *Cf. Mark 9:12; Matt 11:10; 17:11; Luke 7:27; also Luke 1:8–17, 67–69.*

---

4 Kaiser, *Malachi*, 108–9.

- Might the Old Testament Elijah return prior to Christ's second coming?
  - *Not personally (most probably), but the message of the gospel will go forth in the spirit and the power of Elijah prior to Christ's second coming. (Note: this answer is a subject of debate, depending upon one's view of the second coming of Christ.)*
- **Verse 6:** "And he will turn the hearts of fathers to their children and the hearts of children to their fathers, lest I come and strike the land with a decree of utter destruction."
  - Do you think that this restoration (turning) is speaking of a literal millennium (thousand-year reign of Christ on earth)?
  - As for the meaning of this verse, commentators Keil and Delitsch believe the following:[5]
    - The fathers = Israelite fathers/forefathers who are godly
    - The sons/children = the disobedient line of descendants
    - To "turn the hearts of fathers to their children" means to place the fathers' godly affections into the children's hearts.
    - To "turn . . . the hearts of children to their fathers" means the sons/children become likeminded with their pious fathers/forefathers.
  - Walter Kaiser believes that a generation gap occurred after the first restoration to Jerusalem (538 BC), such that the returning remnant never exhibited the faith and faithfulness of their forefathers.[6]
  - Did Israel return to the faith of their fathers when Christ came the first time? *No.* Therefore, when did the curse come to Israel? *The curse came in AD 70 and brought the destruction of Jerusalem by Rome.*

Conclusion

Looking back at the study of Malachi, what was one particular lesson that was impressed upon your mind and heart?

---

5. Keil and Delitzsch, *Commentary on Old Testament*, 472.
6. Kaiser, *Malachi*, 109.

Bibliography

Anderson, Lorin W., and David R. Krathwohl, eds. *A Taxonomy for Learning, Teaching, and Assessing: A Revision of Bloom's Taxonomy of Educational Objectives*. New York: Longman, 2001.

Atherton, J. S. "Learner, Subject and Teacher (3)." Doceo, 2013. http://www.doceo.co.uk/tools/subtle_3.htm.

Bloom, Benjamin, ed. *Taxonomy of Educational Objectives: The Classification of Educational Goals*. New York: McKay, 1965.

Bruce, F. F. *The Epistles of John*. Grand Rapids: Eerdmans, 1970.

Kaiser, Walter C., Jr. *Malachi: God's Unchanging Love*. Grand Rapids: Baker, 1984.

Keil, C. F., and F. Delitzsch. Vol. 10 of *Commentary on the Old Testament*. Grand Rapids: Eerdmans, 1978.

Kennedy, D. James. *Evangelism Explosion*. Wheaton, IL: Tyndale House, 1996.

McKenzie, Jamie. "A Questioning Toolkit." *Now On: The Educational Technology Journal*. 7, no. 3 (Nov.–Dec. 1997). http://www.fno.org/nov97/toolkit.html.

Nicholas, David. *Whatever Happened to the Gospel?* Bloomington, IN: Crossbooks, 2010.

Stott, John, R. W. *The Epistles of John: An Introduction and Commentary*. Tyndale New Testament Commentaries. Grand Rapids: Eerdmans, 1980.

Studd, C. T. "Only One Life, 'Twill Soon Be Past." http://cavaliersonly.com/poetry_by_christian_poets_of_the_past/only_one_life_twill_soon_be_past_-_poem_by_ct_studd.

Traina, Robert A. *Methodological Bible Study*. Grand Rapids: Zondervan, 1952.

Westcott, Brooke Foss. *The Epistles of St. John*. Grand Rapids: Eerdmans, 1966.

Wolf, Herbert M. *Haggai and Malachi: Rededication and Renewal*. Everyman's Bible Commentary. Chicago: Moody, 1976.